DYNAMICS OF CHURCH GROWTH

RON JENSON & JIM STEVENS

BAKER BOOK HOUSE
Grand Rapids, Michigan 49506

Copyright 1981 by
Baker Book House Company

ISBN: 0-8010-5161-4

Printed in the United States of America
This book is in audio tape and notebook form, as well as in correspondence-course form, by Dr. Jenson. For information, contact Great Commission Book Store, International School of Theology, Arrowhead Springs, San Bernardino, CA 92414.

This material is also provided in video form through the National Institute of Biblical Studies, 4001 North Dixie Highway #204, Pompano Beach, FL 33064.

To
Lil, Sue, and Shelley
Mary, Matt, and Molly

Contents

Acknowledgments

We appreciate and are thankful for a number of people who and experiences that have made this book possible. Therefore, we wish to acknowledge:

the work of Campus Crusade for Christ Lay Ministry;

Donald McGavran, C. Peter Wagner, John Wimber, Carl George, and the Charles E. Fuller Institute of Evangelism and Church Growth for their pioneering work in this area, as well as for the many diagnostic tools that are available from the institute;

Dan Reeves, for his initial research and his study of the fifteen principles of church growth;

various parachurch organizations, particularly Campus Crusade for Christ and its president, Dr. Bill Bright, for teaching us about some of those fifteen principles, as well as teaching us the importance of the Spirit of God's work in the local church and in the believer — living by faith, the value of a holy lifestyle, and the value of aggressive evangelism;

the Church of the Saviour, in Wayne, Pennsylvania, its pastors (especially Bill Hogan), its elders, and its people, for supplying us with a living and vital laboratory for cultivating the fifteen principles;

the pastors and other people (especially Carl Combs) affiliated with the Christian Leadership Training Center in Philadelphia, where we worked with as many as seventy-five pastors a week, from twenty-three denominations;

the people who helped us with the manuscript: Rayna Elmendorf and Marc Chandler, for their assistance to Dr. Jenson; Dan Van't Kerkhoff, editor at Baker Book House, who stimulated and encouraged us; and Linda Triemstra, the project editor.

Church Growth:
The Biblical Perspective

A principle fundamental to all of life is that living organisms grow. Growth is a natural, spontaneous expression of life. The only way to stop growth is through disease or death. For example, a mother usually does not worry about whether her new baby will grow. She assumes the child will grow and her primary concern is with her child's health. Health affects development and growth.

The church of Jesus Christ is primarily a living organism and secondarily an organization. Everything about the church involves life. Jesus Christ, the head of the church, is a living Savior. The church includes individuals who have been made alive spiritually as a result of the new birth (John 3:3; Eph. 2:1– 3). Both individually and corporately the church is inhabited by a living Spirit (John 14; I Cor. 3:16– 17), and its affairs are governed by a living book (Heb. 4:12). Since the church pulsates with the life of Christ, we expect the church to grow, unless growth is inhibited by disease. To decide that God does not want us, as churches, to grow means that we have decided to die. There is no other choice, because living things grow. The church has grown since its birth on the day of Pentecost. It had to grow because it was alive.

The study of church growth and the analysis of the dynamics behind how churches grow have received impetus through the work of Donald McGavran and his colleagues at the Fuller Theological Seminary School

9

of World Missions. Their worldwide study of growing churches is valuable in determining the biblical principles necessary to maintain health and thereby guarantee growth. Their study has stimulated interest in church growth. Today church growth is increasingly discussed both in seminaries and in congregations. Pastors are hungry for knowledge about how to regain or maintain the health of their churches. Since church health is the fundamental issue, the church-growth movement focuses on the diagnostic aspect and provides tools to help churches determine the state of their health.

Defining Church Growth

Since interest in church growth is developing rapidly in America, it is important to define this concept of growth. We are not attempting to define the science of church growth or the church-growth movement itself, but rather to define church growth as it relates to individual, local bodies of believers. Church growth is the *balanced increase in quantity, quality, and organizational complexity of a local church.* This definition is the key to understanding the process by which a church grows. If the three components of the increase do not take place in a balanced way, a church will not maintain its good health. If, for example, church growth occurs only as numerical increase, at the expense of quality and organizational development, an unhealthy mutation will develop in a formerly healthy body. The church will be playing the "numbers game." Consequently, the only criteria to evaluate effectiveness will be "how many came?" or "how many indicated decisions?" C. Peter Wagner, in *Your Church Can Grow,* emphasizes the balance of quantitative and qualitative growth when he states that church growth is "all that is involved in bringing men and women that do not have a personal relationship with Jesus Christ into fellowship with Him and into responsible church membership."[1] Evangelism and discipleship, therefore, are parts of *one* process; quantitative and qualitative growth must develop simultaneously and in good balance.

Conversely, if qualitative development excludes quantitative growth, the product is again an unhealthy mutation. The "we're not interested in numbers, only in quality" argument is fallacious. The result is an

1. C. Peter Wagner, *Your Church Can Grow* (Glendale, CA: Regal Books, 1976), p. 12.

ingrown, introspective attitude that not only fails to attract new people, but also repels those who remain. Some churches that place the greatest emphasis on Bible teaching and deeper life are among the smallest and deadest. The problem is not the emphasis, but the imbalance.

Likewise, if organizational and structural development is neglected while the church focuses on quantity and quality, growth will be limited. New people attracted to the church will not be effectively absorbed into the fellowship because of the lack of leadership development and programs to meet their needs. On the other hand, if organization is emphasized without careful attention to quantity and quality, the church will be indistinguishable from the average social club. The church may function well, but it will lack drawing power and spiritual energy.

Examining the Components of a Growing Church

We recognize that the three components of church growth must balance each other. We now look more closely at those components.

Quantitative Growth

Quantitative or numerical growth is implied in the Great Commission of our Lord (Matt. 28:18– 20). The intent of the commission is reflected in the phrase *make disciples.* The verb is supported by three action words—*go, baptize,* and *teach.* This passage could be translated as, "having gone, having baptized, having taught, make disciples." Evangelism precedes teaching, just as birth precedes growth. A church grows in numbers primarily, although not exclusively, when its people witness to those outside the church. This was clearly the practice of the early church, as reported in the Book of Acts. Numbers are mentioned frequently. This individual and corporate passion for extending the gospel message into the whole world, in ever-widening circles of influence, serves as the pattern for the contemporary church to follow. If the church is reaching out, more people will be attracted to its life.

This desire for numerical growth is biblical. The method for accommodating this kind of growth will vary from church to church. Some churches will develop into "superchurches," whereas others will choose to develop "daughter" churches and to expand numerically by division. Whatever method is adopted, the attitude and desire must be to see increasing numbers of people coming into a relationship with Christ and being absorbed into the life of His body, the church.

Qualitative Growth

Acts 2:42– 43 describes people who were growing qualitatively in their relationship to Christ and to one another. This growth was reflected in the "awe" (v. 43) that enveloped the church and community as the believers observed what God was doing. Qualitative growth is the progressive development of the body into the likeness of its head, Jesus Christ. As the church grows, it will become increasingly Christ-like in its corporate behavior and character.

One barometer, which is repeatedly emphasized in the New Testament and helps gauge growth into Christ-likeness, is the quality of unity. It is a significant indicator. Unity is impossible to attain from human efforts because of the diversity of ages, backgrounds, personalities, and gifts within the church. Unity indicates that God is mightily at work and the body is developing qualitatively. Such growth occurs as believers are exposed to excellent teaching and are given opportunities to apply scriptural principles within the family, the church, and the world.

Problems, such as gossip, slander, and other actions strictly forbidden in the New Testament, devastate many churches. These churches are not growing qualitatively. The tragedy is not only the toll such behavior takes in the church itself, but also the degree to which such churches lose their power to attract members. The life of Christ, demonstrated in the observable love and unity of a church, is like a powerful magnet which the Holy Spirit uses to attract those who do not know Christ. The lack of qualitative growth is detrimental to quantitative growth. The two cannot be separated. We realize this from the years we spent in ministering to students. We were amazed to see how little effect the church had on many students who had been reared under its influence. These students were indifferent to their churches because they did not see a genuineness of life. They did not experience the awe that comes from observing Jesus Christ at work in a powerful way through the body of believers.

Organic Growth

Organic growth is reflected in the organizational and structural development of a church. A church must effectively absorb new people into its life. As the number of members grows, so must the organization. A church is a complex organism because it must meet diverse needs. Many churches stop growing numerically at a certain point because they do not develop sufficient, capable leadership to serve the new members. A church with two thousand members has an organizational chart that looks unbelievably complex compared to a chart for a church with two hundred members. For growth to continue, a church must be willing to change its structure.

Churches tend to let their organizational and management structures fossilize. As growth occurs, full-time and part-time staff should be added, new facilities built, new ministries developed and staffed, and other changes made as needs dictate. Sometimes we consider management and management training in a negative way, but they are vital if a church is to grow. When a church stops growing organically it will stop growing qualitatively and quantitatively as well.

Sustaining the Health of a Growing Church

To sustain the health of a church, three factors are involved: focusing on a biblical product; maintaining biblical presuppositions; and following biblical principles.

Focusing on a Biblical Product

A product is the result of a process. In every area of life, especially with regard to the church, it is essential for Christians to maintain a perspective and a mental image of what God wants them to become. To do this, we must first find what characteristics a church has when it is fully developed and functioning biblically. Most of us do not know from firsthand experience, but the New Testament has much to say about this.

We easily get lost in the process without a clear idea of what we are trying to become (the product). This results in perpetual crisis management and a deadly drift from program to program, without a sense of direction and purpose. If individual members of the ruling body in the average church were asked to write out their visions of what their church should be twenty years from now, these people would express divergent opinions. Most of us fail to think seriously about it.

Ephesians 4:11–16 (a passage to which we will refer repeatedly in this book) gives a composite picture of the ideal, healthy church. Its three basic concepts comprise a biblical product.

The healthy church has a broad view of leadership (vv. 11– 12). These verses tell us that God has given gifted men, with specific responsibilities, to the church. The pastors/teachers are to "prepare God's people for works of service" (v. 12). The full-time leadership of the local body must assist laymen to do (and do well) what God has called and gifted them to do. A pastor's purpose is not to perform all the work, but to effectively develop others' leadership and service capabilities. Many pastors become extremely frustrated because their congregations expect them to possess all the gifts. A healthy church, on the other hand, recognizes the proper role of leadership and works to develop lay leadership accordingly. A church will grow only when leadership is developed.

The healthy church develops a certain kind of person and body. A healthy church has a Christ-likeness of behavior and character (vv. 13– 15), which includes the qualities of unity, love, stability, and maturity that ultimately result in "... attaining the full measure of perfection found in Christ" (v. 13). We look at Jesus Christ and long to be like Him. This is the aim and the result of the "equipping" of verse 12 (NASB). Equipping calls for men in our pulpits who possess a personal passion for God—men who exemplify Christ-like qualities and are able to equip their people to have the same qualities. Equipping is more than placing people into functional jobs in the church. It means that a visitor walking into church should sense in the pastor, as well as in the people, love, a sense of belonging, and a genuineness of life. He should sense a preoccupation with Jesus Christ.

The healthy church fosters a ministry that is structured around the involvement of its members. This characteristic follows from the first two. A healthy church is an active body. Its members are serving. The pews are filled with involved people. A good sign of health is a high percentage of the members involved in at least one ministry. A church whose members are being led—through teaching, modeling, and training—to be like Christ will take on more and more of Christ's attitude about serving. Through seeing others serve, new members should sense that it is normal and natural to find their own places of service within the body. The church grows as "each part does its work" (v. 16).

These three features of a healthy church form the composite picture of gifted men leading people into service and a full-orbed walk with Christ, which results in building up the body of Christ (vv. 12, 16).

Maintaining Biblical Presuppositions

A second factor in promoting a healthy church is the maintenance of biblical presuppositions. These four presuppositions must be kept in focus if church health is to be sustained.

The church will want to grow. Many churches do not want to grow. Some church members fear that "if we grow, things will not be as they are now." Such people fear that if their church grows they will lose the intimacy of their fellowship. This fear, whether unspoken or spoken, creates an aversion to growth that squelches vision and motivation. In many churches, some people want growth and others do not. Or a pastor may not want church growth and consequently fails to enlarge the vision of his people. Where the status quo becomes the norm, no spark exists to ignite growth. When this spark goes out, fatal disease sets in, and the church slips into the process of slow death.

The church will be willing to pay the price. Growth exacts a price—in money, time, and facility development. Church members must decide that "we will do whatever is necessary, within biblical guidelines, to grow." This will have various implications. For example, some intimacy will be lost for the sake of ministering to more people. Deliberate sin cannot be tolerated because sin is disease, and a diseased body cannot grow. Long-range planning must recognize and provide for the needs of new members. If a desire to grow does not exist, there will be no willingness to do whatever is necessary to grow and stay healthy.

The church will not have a terminal illness. [2] Growth will not occur without good health. Disease, if not checked, will ultimately be fatal. It is painful to watch a church trying to die gracefully. Many pastors are presiding over the deaths of churches. In a subsequent chapter, we will enumerate several common diseases and show their effects.

The church will follow certain priorities. Figure 1 helps to illustrate those priorities. The space outside the circles indicates the world. God has called us to extend the message of reconciliation to the whole world. Our local churches can affect the whole world. The Lord will call church members to go to the ends of the earth. Our money can support missions throughout the world. We are part of God's plan for illuminating the whole world with the gospel.

We are not, however, going to influence the world—especially our

2. Wagner, *Your Church Can Grow,* pp. 124– 146.

Figure 1

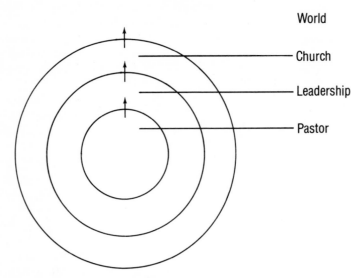

piece of it—as we should until the local church pulsates with spiritual life and exhibits a corporate lifestyle that attracts people to Christ. The way to reach the world is through healthy local churches.

To change the world we must change churches, and to change churches we must change leadership. Leadership is basic to church health. People are challenged primarily by observing good examples. Such examples create a hunger to live by commitment and loyalty. Also, good leadership equips the saints by teaching and training them. Pastors and lay leaders, however, cannot teach love and unity without demonstrating those qualities among themselves. If leaders do not take this responsibility seriously, they will find themselves presiding over a collection of programs instead of guiding a living, dynamic organism.

To strengthen lay leadership we must have strong pastors. The lay leaders will be only as strong as the equipper. What we have said about leadership is especially true of the pastor. He bears a primary responsibility to display vision, life, and passion for God.

These qualities flow from pastor to leadership to churches to the world. Disease within any part will prevent effectiveness in the next. A church does not automatically affect the world in a positive way. It can do so only when the people at each level—pastors, leaders, members—maintain their spiritual health.

Following Biblical Principles

Biblical principles are fundamental to church growth, and we will examine fifteen of those principles. Note that we do not say that church health depends on following certain forms of ministry. A form or method is only a way to apply the principle. Generally, forms cannot be transferred from one culture to another, but principles are transferable. Consider two churches that are growing rapidly. One might be an inner-city church in a blue-collar area and the other a predominately suburban congregation. The form, methods, emphases, and programs may vary greatly between the two churches. But beneath the varied forms of ministry you will find the same principles in operation.

Principles of church growth are clarified by looking through three lenses. The first is the lens of Scripture, the second is the lens of history, and the third is the lens of the contemporary local situation. If a church uses these three perspectives, principles emerge which, if followed, result in health. Health in turn results in natural growth. A church does not merely try to grow. It should first determine what it must do to stay healthy.

The fifteen principles listed below will operate cross-culturally and will cut across social classes. To apply them will require different methodologies for different situations. No single plan will work in each case. But all the principles must operate in every case if a church is to grow. Each principle is listed with a descriptive phrase to assist the memory.

Principle	*Descriptive phrase*
1. Prayer	ask and expect God to do the miraculous
2. Worship	experience meaningful corporate celebration
3. Purpose	unite around common objectives
4. Diagnosis	analyze the local church and the community
5. Priorities	emphasize important activities and values
6. Planning	project ways to achieve objectives
7. Programming	build ministries which move toward objectives
8. Climate	radiate love, service, witness, and expectancy
9. Leadership	motivate and guide toward objectives
10. Laity	utilize the strengths of individuals
11. Absorption	establish a strong sense of belonging
12. Small Groups	develop deep interpersonal relationships
13. Discipleship	promote commitment and spiritual multiplication
14. Training	equip with knowledge, skills, and character
15. Evangelism	present the gospel effectively

Each chapter of this book will discuss one of these principles, including its implications. Each principle will be explained in relation to the three types of growth (quantitative, qualitative, and organic) listed in our definition. Tools for applying the principles will be presented (Action Items), along with a brief bibliography, at the end of each chapter. Unless otherwise indicated, all Scripture references are from the *Holy Bible: New International Version,* copyright 1978 by the New York International Bible Society.

1

Prayer

The quantitative, qualitative, and organic increase in a local body of believers is a supernatural process. The church is God's creation, and Jesus Christ is its head. Life flows from His indwelling presence, and growth occurs as a result of that divine life. The church is a living organism. It develops and grows through a Godmade, not a manmade, process. In I Corinthians 3, Paul dealt with division in the church. Apollos had his following and Paul had his. In describing the ultimate responsibility for church growth, Paul wrote, "I planted the seed, Apollos watered it, but God made it grow" (I Cor. 3:6). Paul placed the ultimate responsibility where it belonged and recognized the supernaturalness of the growth process. He recognized that after all human effort had been expended, lasting growth depended on God. A seed can be planted and the growing plant watered, pruned, and cared for; but growth is a result of a supernatural, mysterious, and wonderful process that takes place underground, independent of human will or hands. So it is with the church. Who can explain how a person is transferred from the kingdom of darkness to the kingdom of God's beloved Son (Col. 1:14)? Who can explain the process by which a person develops in Christlikeness? The psalmist stated, "Unless the Lord builds the house, its builders labor in vain" (Ps. 127:1). Although labor may progress, it is in vain if God is not blessing it. Such labor has no lasting results or benefits. We can paraphrase this verse, apply it to church growth, and not lose the important principle: unless the Lord builds the church, those who organize it, program it, and finance it do so in vain. Until we recognize the supernaturalness of the process and see human effort in perspective, nothing of lasting value can be accomplished. We, of ourselves, cannot make the church grow.

Lasting Growth Depends on God

Too often, those of us involved in the great adventure of church development tend to take the credit for accomplishments that God brought about. Many times people ask, "Why is your church growing so fast?" Often our answer tends to credit man's efforts. We may think for a minute and then credit our success to a superb staff, to financial resources, or to strong pastoral leadership. Without minimizing the extent to which God uses man's involvement, the answer to the question is, simply, "God." Churches built around the great preaching talents of one man or the organizational abilities of another need to resist the temptation to credit the man with growth. At best we are planters and waterers. God supplies the life and growth. He must receive the credit.

How does this relate to prayer? If we are convinced that growth comes from God and is therefore supernatural, and if we are equally convinced that we are dependent on Him for lasting results, then prayer will be at the top of our corporate priority list. If God causes growth, then we must be in touch with Him. If we are not, we labor in vain, spinning our wheels in a flurry of spiritual activity without the corresponding spiritual results. It is not enough for our spiritual machine to be well-oiled. Genuine spiritual change will occur only in answer to prayer, as we learn to depend on Him. The focus must shift from ourselves to God. If our adequacy is from God and not from ourselves, then our focus must be on Him as the resource from which we must draw our strength.

The Holy Spirit's Role in Church Growth

To be convinced that the source of growth is God and that human effort is futile without His blessing, we must understand the role of the Holy Spirit in the church. In looking at two specific ways in which the

Holy Spirit operates with respect to the church, we will clearly understand who is responsible for church growth.

The Holy Spirit Establishes the Church

There would be no church without the work of the Holy Spirit. The Holy Spirit brings people into the church. Colossians 1:14 makes it clear that we have been transferred from the old kingdom to a new kingdom. We have changed kingdoms, or spheres, of spiritual life. This change took place because of the work of the Holy Spirit. He brings about this transfer through a three-step process.

The Holy Spirit establishes the church as He *convicts*. The definitive passage about this vital ministry of the Spirit is John 16:8-11. Jesus said that when the Spirit came He would "convict the world concerning sin, and righteousness, and judgment ..." (v. 8, NASB). In another passage, John 6:44, Jesus said that "No one can come to me unless the Father who sent me draws him. ..." Conviction is the divine approach whereby God begins, in a mysterious way, to draw, soften, and create an awareness of need in a hardened heart. It is amazing how two people can react to the same presentation of the gospel message. Many times we have shared the gospel with one person and have seen an apathetic or openly antagonistic response, only to go on to another and observe a tearful, broken, and glad response to the same message. The difference is that in some unseen way, beyond our control, God's Spirit has used another witness—a piece of literature, a death in the family, or some other means—to soften the heart, to open spiritual eyes, and to bring a deep sense of need. Many times we have come away from observing spiritual birth with an awesome appreciation of having seen God at work deep in the heart and conscience of another person. To think that our training, skill, or knowledge is responsible for conviction is a serious error in judgment. The Spirit will employ human resources in His work, but the responsibility (and credit) for convicting a person is His alone.

The second step in the Holy Spirit's work is *conversion*. Conversion is the fruit of conviction. It is conviction carried to the point of decision. In a way we will never understand or be able to explain, the Holy Spirit draws us and creates in us an awareness of our deep need. He then gives us the ability to believe the gospel message and to place our trust in Him. He causes the transfer to take place. Titus 3:5 describes the process as the "... washing of rebirth and renewal by the Holy Spirit. ..." The crucial point is that we, as sinners, have nothing to do with our conversion. Nor do evangelists have anything to do with conversion in the life of another.

We recall the joy of observing the Holy Spirit lead a business executive through the conviction and conversion process. The first human approach to this man was a neighborhood visitation call. In his living room we explained the gospel message to him and his wife. As a career engineer he was apathetic, skeptical, and saw an immediate conflict between the Christian message and his scientific training. We left, on cordial terms, not really expecting anything to develop. We did decide, however, to invite him and his wife to an evangelistic dinner where a professional athlete was the speaker. To our delight, they came and seemed to enjoy the evening. A few weeks later we invited him to attend an evangelistic breakfast, where he heard another gifted speaker. After that, he was visibly affected by the message and soon came to faith in Christ. He and his wife now faithfully attend our church and are growing into the likeness of Christ.

This experience is similar to thousands of other evangelistic experiences. The Holy Spirit, using an initial human contact, a piece of literature, or a television broadcast, begins to convict the sinner, to draw him, and to soften his heart. Usually several contacts occur, until the Holy Spirit moves the person to a point of decision and conversion. The transfer is complete and another person is a member of God's eternal family. In an unexplainable and unseen way God's Spirit worked to move a person from apathy and antagonism into membership in God's family.

The third ingredient of the Holy Spirit's work, in addition to conviction and conversion, is *confession*. These three ingredients are parts of one process and are results of God's Spirit at work in individual hearts. In I Corinthians 12:3 we read, "... no one can say, 'Jesus is Lord,' except by the Holy Spirit." The Holy Spirit causes conversion and then enables the person to verbalize his commitment to Christ.

Are we really convinced that evangelistic results are the work of God, that we are simply mouthpieces, and that God's Word is strangely and wonderfully used by the Spirit to bring about the transfer from the old kingdom to the new? If we are convinced, will that not dramatically affect our corporate and individual prayer for our communities, neighbors, and friends who do not know Christ? Too often, evangelistic planning and activity in our churches are man-centered rather than God-centered. In our church, we have noticed that those evangelistic activities preceded by concentrated prayer invariably are well-planned, well-attended, and exceptionally fruitful. This is no accident. It follows naturally, since God is responsible for establishing the church.

The Holy Spirit Equips the Church

In addition to establishing the church, the Holy Spirit equips the church. Equipping is the gradual development into Christ-likeness. The Holy Spirit not only causes people to enter the church but He also directs the growth of these individuals, and the church corporately, into Christ-likeness. Sometimes it seems easy to depend on the Lord for the evangelization of our communities, but it seems much more difficult to depend on the Lord for the growth that follows. It is as if we say to the Lord, "You get them in and we'll take over from there and cause them to grow." We need to be convinced that we are no more able to cause growth than we are able to cause conversion. Galatians 5:22 describes nine qualities of Christ-like behavior and character as the fruit of spiritual growth. Paul calls this fruit the "fruit of the Spirit." In other words, the fruit originates not from the man in whom it occurs, but from the Spirit who lives within. This occurs within the individual who is within the corporate body of Christ. This production of fruit—the changes in attitude and habit that are occurring *internally* in the individual—is caused by the Holy Spirit. Ephesians 3:16 says this activity of the Spirit occurs in the "inner man." If the Holy Spirit lives within a man, He is at work in that man. He is moving, changing, guiding, and developing that man into Christ's likeness. Many adolescents often hear remarks like, "You know, the older you get, the more you look like your dad." That points out a rich truth. The Holy Spirit inside of us says, "You know, the older you get, the more you look like Jesus." The process may appear slow at times, but the timetable is His, as well as the work. Philippians 1:6 tells us that the one who began the work in us will perform it until the day Jesus Christ returns. The Holy Spirit equips the church, or develops it into Christ-likeness, in three major ways.

The Holy Spirit equips the church through the use of the Word of God. Hebrews 4:12 describes the Word of God as living, active, and sharp. In John 16:13 we read that the Spirit "... will guide you into all truth." Truth about what? Truth about Jesus Christ. The context of this passage is the discourse in which Jesus is dealing with His confused, discouraged disciples. Their questions to Him (in John 14) relate to His relationship to God, the kingdom, and themselves. One of the ministries of the Comforter, Jesus told them, would be to take the blinders from their spiritual eyes and lead them into a depth of understanding about

Himself—Jesus Christ, the Son. The Holy Spirit came to glorify the Son. The instrument He uses is the written Word of God. The living Spirit takes the living Word, energizes it, and in a mysterious, supernatural way uses it to change a person on the inside—the inner man. In I Thessalonians 2:13, Paul talks about the Word "performing its work" in those who believe.

Not only does the Holy Spirit use the Word, but He also uses people in proclaiming and unfolding the meaning of the Word. According to Ephesians 4:12, God has given gifted men to the church to "prepare God's people for works of service." How many times have we seen men and women who were spiritually dead come into God's family and blossom as they learned from the ministry of the Word as proclaimed by a gifted preacher or teacher? The Spirit performs a miracle of life before our eyes. Sometimes a minister spends hours preparing a sermon, but after delivering it discovers that people were blessed and challenged in unexpected ways. The minister may have made practical suggestions for applying the truth, only to have someone find an application that he had never thought of before. This indicates that the Spirit is at work using the exposition of the Word for "teaching, rebuking, correcting and training . . ." (II Tim. 3:16– 17).

The Holy Spirit uses the minister to explain the meaning of the Word. But the Spirit Himself is at work on a deeper level, using the Word to bring about change. Who then is responsible for growth incurred by the preaching of the Word? Is it the minister? No. We must direct the credit and glory to God. We must not give man credit for results that do not belong to him. If we are convinced that God is responsible, how will our prayer lives be affected? If we believe this, the quantity and quality of our prayers should radically change.

The third way the Spirit equips the church is by granting spiritual gifts to individual believers. Have you ever considered what an ingenious concept a spiritual gift is? If you had to bring scores of people together in one group, given the diversity of ages, backgrounds, and spiritual maturity, how would you do it? How would you structure the ministry of that body so that its objective is accomplished while love and unity prevail? The New Testament has scores of exhortations about unity because God knew that unity would be the hardest quality to maintain in a diverse group. To solve this problem, God planned to give every believer a spiritual gift to fill a special role in the church. Each gift should contribute something to the total body. This is the secret of unity. Discord in the church is the clearest indication that individuals are not operating in their Spirit-given areas of service. When people begin to function in their God-given roles, disunity will disappear because criticism and jealousy are no longer necessary. It is amazing how different the members of our church staff are from each other. In spite of these differences, unity prevails because they are not trying to do what God has called the others to do. Each of us has limitations, but God has given abilities to others to compensate for our limitations. No one person is a superman. Each member has a unique capability. We must exercise our gifts, not belittle or flaunt them. We invite disunity when we begin to compare ourselves with others and dwell on other people's limitations. Believers must depend on the Lord and recognize a complementary relationship with each other. This is the genius of the church.

Parachurch organizations—with limited objectives and tasks to perform in the wider context of the universal body of Christ—sometimes encounter difficulty in attracting and holding large numbers of diverse people. In the ministry of parachurch organizations, believers may not exercise a wide range of gifts. Members of these organizations sometimes wonder why people leave their groups. Because people can be best fulfilled when they are exercising their God-given abilities, a group in which everyone is expected to do the same thing may experience rapid turnover. The local church specifically can provide believers a chance for the full expression of spiritual gifts. God intended it to be so.

This principle was revealed in one of our Bible-study groups, which was on the verge of collapse. The leader was a godly man. He was an effective host, a good listener, and open to suggestions. He was not, however, a good teacher and study leader. We suggested that another man, who had the gift of teaching, should lead the Bible study. Soon the attendance increased, and both men were fulfilled. As long as both men were not functioning according to their God-given abilities, the ministry floundered. The same phenomenon occurs repeatedly in our church, and it is not controlled or manipulated by man. It is a God-directed process.

How will knowing this truth affect our corporate prayer lives? We will bathe every recruiting drive in prayer. We will ask, "Is this person supernaturally endowed to do this job?" rather than, "Is this person available?" Sometimes we do not know a person's gift until he experiments with a number of jobs in the church. But, if given the chance, each person will find a place of service that he alone can fill because it is a unique niche that the Holy Spirit created for him.

Implications of the Holy Spirit's Ministries

We turn now to the implications of these ministries of the Holy Spirit—establishing and equipping the church. These implications influence our faith and the way we pray.

Implications for Prayer

If we are to see quantitative, qualitative, and organic growth of the church, we must take prayer much more seriously than we have in the past. God loves His church. He stands ready to make His resources available to us. But He sometimes waits for us to ask. These words sound so logical and theologically correct, yet they are so difficult to put into practice. We stubbornly continue to think we are able to run our churches well on our own resources, without recognizing the divine impetus. We lack a deep sense of needing to depend on God. We do it so well by ourselves, we think. We know how to program creatively so there are activities for every age. We know how to communicate theological abstractions in an appealing way. We know how to build beautiful and expensive facilities to house our programs. We know how to transfer corporate structure into the church so the organization is superb. We know how to do these things, and we think they can be done without God. In many of our churches, if God removed Himself from the picture nothing would change. The lack of a sense of needing God diminishes our sense of need to pray. Anemic corporate prayer reflects our lack of understanding about the supernatural processes at work in church growth.

We talk about prayer in the abstract, but we do not make it our number-one priority. Such apathy toward prayer may be the result of our tendency to measure results in a different way than God does. Our measuring devices reveal the number of people, the amount of dollars, or the facilities. Although God is also concerned about the external aspects of the church, He measures results in a different way. He looks at the condition of men's hearts. He is concerned about unconfessed sin, whether we love Him and each other, whether we care about those who are lost—things which He alone can deal with in answer to prayer. It is possible to have a successful church as we measure success and yet be failures according to God's standards. It is easy to promote campaigns for more people and dollars, or to build bigger facilities. On the other hand, we cannot create repentant hearts, genuine love for one another, or spiritual growth. God is at work beneath the surface of men's hearts and lives. He is moving where human manipulation and promotion cannot penetrate. Paul gave us models for our prayers. He constantly prayed that his people develop those spiritual qualities that are of paramount importance. He prayed for deepening love between believers, for a clearer understanding of who Jesus is, and for increased patience in tribulation and persecution. When we begin to see that nothing that matters will occur except in answer to prayer, then prayer will become more than an optional program for the faithful few, and instead will become the driving force of our churches.

Implications for Faith

The Holy Spirit's work in church growth also has implications for our faith. Too many of us accept the status quo. We have entered into a "ministry of maintenance." There is a strange lack of a bold trust in God to do the miraculous. We have become a timid generation. We have come to consider God incapable of doing "great and unsearchable things" (Jer. 33:3).

Part of our inability to trust God is that we do not have a strong sense of need. We will trust God only when we have to. We tend to look for every human alternative or solution to a problem before we finally turn to God. To teach the disciples the great lessons about faith, Jesus repeatedly brought them into situations that were hopeless from a human point of view—the storm on the sea, or five thousand people without food. He was training them to turn to Him instinctively with an attitude of dependence and expectancy. We will learn to turn to Him as they did only when we come to see the futility of trying to produce spiritual results apart from Him.

Our lack of expectancy and bold faith can be traced directly to our misunderstanding of who is responsible for the growth of the church. If we believe that growth is manmade, then we will look to man for the resources. Our focus will be on manmade plans and strategies. We will look for human solutions to insoluble problems. But the result of a manmade process is a manmade product, which does not last. The church was not designed to run with man at the controls. If the church is to grow it must be dependent on God. If it is dependent, it will also be expectant. The whole process will become the great adventure it was meant to be: the adventure of seeing the living God regularly doing things that cannot be explained in human terms. If we know that only

God can make things happen, then we will ask Him for the impossible and believe that He will do it.

Knowing that only God can do the impossible will cause us to pray with a certain kind of faith. It will be a faith that *aims* and a faith that *acts*.

What are we aiming for in our churches? Are we setting goals that can be reached only if God does something? Are we praying and setting goals both for the tangible things such as attendance and giving and for the intangible and subjective things such as love for the lost? What do you want your people to be? What can we trust God for? In learning to pray and to believe God will provide the intangible, it is helpful to pray for things that can be objectively measured. Part of the problem with our praying is that we would not recognize an answer if God gave it, because we do not pray specifically enough. Observable answers to prayer stimulate further ventures in trusting God for even bigger things.

Christians need to learn how to pray and work toward *faith events*. Faith events challenge God's people to believe He will provide something beyond their reach. They develop a capacity and momentum for trusting God increasingly for something bigger than they can accomplish. For example, when we started a singles ministry in our church, one of the programs featured music, discussion groups, and drama. At first, the leadership prayed for one hundred people to attend. One hundred people is not very many, but to this small group it seemed like a thousand. This was a faith-stretching goal, since one hundred people would come only if God did something out of the ordinary. There were no human resources for attracting that many people. God answered, and 140 people attended the first meeting. Encouraged, the leadership prayed for a larger number the next time. Every time a new faith goal was set, corporate faith was strengthened. The small group of single people was ignited. Nothing will ignite a group more than seeing bona fide answers to prayer. Everyone needed to recognize that we could not have done it by human effort—that only God could have done it.

At another time, we were trying to raise $500,000 in one night for the second phase of our building program. We had prayed for weeks toward that end. From a human standpoint, it was an impossible goal. Our people were already giving generously. Only God could do it. On that evening, after the pledges had been counted, we received more than $500,000. The atmosphere was charged with spiritual electricity. Why? Because God had done something, and everyone recognized it.

Our churches need to mobilize to pray about faith-stretching goals.

Begin by praying together for seemingly hopeless situations—an alcoholic who needs to be delivered, a family that seems irrevocably divided, or a wayward brother or sister who needs to be restored. Continue to pray for other impossible situations. So many churches are demoralized. They have a "loser mentality." But such churches can change when small groups gather to pray for the impossible. God loves that kind of prayer, and He will respond to it.

Faith not only aims at the impossible, but it also *acts*. Faith is never passive. Faith can visualize the answer as if it had already been given. The great chapter about faith, Hebrews 11, is packed with action words. Faith in the New Testament is always related to works. God acts in response to the faith of His people. Faith involves risks. Faith involves trying without the fear of failure. Faith is uncomfortable. It means Christians must learn to "go out on a limb." It means learning to ignore rejection. For example, when our church was three years old, God led us to a beautiful thirty-acre plot of land. The price for the land seemed astronomical to our small congregation. Some people thought we were insane to consider buying that much land. But God had given us a vision for a certain kind of church, and we believed that He wanted us to trust Him for acquiring that land. At the time three acres would have been sufficient for our needs. But faith looks beyond today's need. We both prayed and acted. We raised the money, purchased the land, and built on it. Three years later, the thirty acres of land does not seem like much at all in light of the explosive growth that has occurred.

Yet another example will illustrate this same principle. When we confront seemingly desperate personal or family problems (such as that of the alcoholic we mentioned before), we need to act as well as to pray. We can help to solve the problem by listening, caring, and offering practical assistance.

However, churches often lack the faith and courage to set goals. Many pastors find it difficult to make faith statements. In fact, setting goals seems to be anathema to many pastors. We think two major reasons account for this reluctance.

The first obstacle is that Christians seem to fear failure or rejection. This is illustrated in the parable of the talents (Matt. 25:25), when the servant told his master that he was afraid to invest the money given to his care lest something happen to it. He was afraid to take a risk. Conversely, Dr. Robert Schuller has stated, "I would rather attempt something great for God and fail than attempt nothing for God and succeed." Another man of faith recently said that we should "attempt something so great that, unless God is in it, it's doomed to failure."

The key to understanding this positive attitude is in our sense of what comprises success and what comprises failure.

Paul says, "But thanks be to God, who always leads us in his triumphal procession in Christ and through us spreads everywhere the fragrance of the knowledge of him. For we are to God the aroma of Christ among those who are being saved and those who are perishing. To the one we are the smell of death; to the other, the fragrance of life. And who is equal to such a task?" (II Cor. 2:14– 16). Paul knew that he was victorious even when people rejected him. Although people laughed at him or criticized his leadership, Paul maintained a constant sense of being triumphant in Christ. That is the way to defeat the fear of failure.

A second hindrance to developing faith statements is a sense of inadequacy. Some pastors feel that no matter what they attempt, they will remain inadequate. Paul spoke about this: "Such confidence as this is ours through Christ before God. Not that we are competent to claim anything for ourselves, but our competence comes from God" (II Cor. 3:4– 5). He knew that his sense of adequacy was not based on what he did, but was rooted in God and who He is. He also knew that he would never be adequate in his own strength to do the task. Every pastor must have that attitude. That is why a pastor can believe God will do great things, and why he can make daring faith statements. Someone has stated, "We don't test the resources of God until we attempt the impossible." That is exactly what God wants us to do — to rely on Him and to test His resources. It is not our great faith in God that causes us to achieve what God wants us to achieve, but our faith in a great God.

God wants our churches, our pastors, and our leaders to recognize that only He can do extraordinary things. When we accept that simple premise, we will begin to pray in a way that will change us. We will pray, because to do anything else will be folly. When we begin to ask God for the impossible, our faith will begin to expand as we watch Him perform what we requested. We will set goals that only He can reach, and we will begin to act as if we believe that God is in charge and will do what we ask. This helps us to develop a positive and expectant attitude. This will bring back the sense of "awe" which was so deeply felt in the early church community (Acts 2:43). Prayer indeed is the foundation for church growth.

Action Item

Evaluate how your pastor and church leaders use corporate prayer. The ratings range from "1" (the minimum) to "5" (the maximum).

	Pastor	Laity
Emphasize prayers of faith.	1 2 3 4 5	1 2 3 4 5
Demonstrate optimistic faith by praying for large numbers of people to come to Christ.	1 2 3 4 5	1 2 3 4 5
Express faith by writing clear objectives for church growth.	1 2 3 4 5	1 2 3 4 5
Experience and tell others about regular answers to prayer.	1 2 3 4 5	1 2 3 4 5
Make prayer a major emphasis of each meeting.	1 2 3 4 5	1 2 3 4 5

Bibliography

Bounds, E. M. *Power Through Prayer.* Grand Rapids: Baker, 1972.

Wagner, C. Peter. *Your Church Can Grow.* Glendale, CA: Regal, 1976.

2
Worship

Whether a healthy church has seventy-five people in attendance or five thousand, it will contain three building blocks, as named and described by Peter Wagner: the *celebration*, the *subcongregation,* and the *cell*. Celebration describes the corporate gathering or worship of the total body. The subcongregation is the celebration as it meets in fellowship and identity groups, such as Sunday-school classes or midweek prayer groups. It is the first line of assimilation into the life of the church. A cell is an even smaller group, and its main purpose is to develop intimacy and accountability.

In this chapter we will focus on the role of the celebration as it relates to the growth of the church in its quantitative and qualitative aspects. Subsequent chapters will examine the roles of the subcongregation and the cell. In dealing with the celebration, we will look at the purpose and definition of worship, its ingredients, and its implications for church growth.

The Definition and Purpose of Worship

Webster defines worship as the "reverent love and allegiance accorded a deity, idol, or sacred object." The Greek words for worship combine the ideas of "falling down before," "paying homage to," and

32

"serving." One of the Greek words evokes a mental picture "of a dog which crouches at its master's feet. Worship, therefore, is an act in which the devout soul prostrates itself before God in humble homage and entire submission."[1] From this definition, it is obvious that worship (a compound word based on the words *worthy* and *ship*) involves the recognition of worth in God, and the offering of our honor, praise, and adoration to the One who is altogether worthy.

This definition leads us to consider the purpose of worship. This consideration is crucial because it strikes at the very purpose of the church. The health of our personal and corporate worship reflects the health of our personal and corporate relationship to God. To worship genuinely is to know God. To know God genuinely is to be in a king/subject relationship with Him. Worship acknowledges His kingship in our lives and His right, as our sovereign Lord, to rule over us. Corporate worship means church members gather to ascribe worth to God. Worship is for God's benefit. He has center stage. I Chronicles 29:11–13 gives us a biblical description and the correct focus of worship:

> Yours, O LORD, is the greatness and the power and the glory and the majesty and the splendor, for everything in heaven and earth is yours. Yours, O LORD, is the kingdom; you are exalted as head over all. Wealth and honor come from you; you are the ruler of all things. In your hands are strength and power to exalt and give strength to all. Now, our God, we give you thanks, and praise your glorious name.

Corporate worship recognizes God's glory, greatness, power, victory, majesty, and dominion. During worship, the body yields itself to the rule and dominion of God. Worship is the bowing of the corporate knee to His authority. It is the body confessing its dependence on God as its sovereign Head.

Many evangelical Christians misunderstand the purpose of corporate worship. Modern worship has become an experience in which man is the focus. Worship has deteriorated into an "I didn't get anything out of the sermon" experience. Man has become the object of his own worship. He is there to be entertained and spiritually massaged. It hardly occurs to some Christians that worship is primarily a matter of God receiving something from us—our praise, adoration, and confession of dependence on Him as our sovereign.

1. Lloyd Perry, *Getting the Church on Target* (Chicago: Moody Press, 1977), p. 210.

The state of worship today is a symptom of the spiritual decay of our generation. What should be a joyous, grand celebration of all that God is has turned into a deadening, ritualistic experience that leaves us just as far from God when we leave the service as we were when we entered. To genuinely worship is to enter the throne room of the King, to pay homage to Him, and to exult in our relationship with Him. Too many Christians, when asked to explain the purpose of the worship service, will say that it is meaningless, that they cannot understand what is happening, or that they dislike the dead ritual. To worship is to be in touch with God—to pray to God, to sing to God, to confess to God, and to respond to God as He has been exalted and revealed in His Word. The purpose is to give something, not to receive something. Blessing will certainly come, but receiving is the result of giving. The great liturgies, developed through the centuries of church history, were designed to lift the heart and spirit in response to God. Unfortunately, this purpose has been lost. The form, the method, and the trappings have been retained, but the reality and sense of joy have been lost for thousands of regular churchgoers. In churches across the land, people walk away from services every Sunday and feel cheated. Many Christians might say that a walk in the woods or by a stream would have drawn them nearer to God than did the service they attended.

Causes of Sterile Worship

This misunderstanding about the real purpose of worship has contributed to sterile corporate worship and has devastated the potential for growth in many churches. Three factors account for our misunderstandings about worship.

Culture

The first reason for lukewarm worship is the culture in which we live. We live at a frantic pace. We live in an "instant" age and society. Television has taught us to expect instant gratification of our every need and desire. Everything worthwhile has to come to us immediately. Patience is a scarce commodity. We find it hard to be patient even when standing in line at a "fast food" restaurant. Somehow it is not fast enough. Surely they could speed it up so we would not have to wait at all. This characteristic of our culture has carried over into our spiritual lives, and particularly into our practice of worship, in insidious ways.

The Bible repeatedly states that we must learn to *wait* on God in order to receive blessing from Him (Pss. 25:5; 37:7; 40:1; Isa. 40:31). To wait does not mean to sit for hours in a yoga position with eyes shut and with the mind neutral. It does mean focusing, quietly and reflectively, on God. It necessitates disengaging the mind from the cares, frustrations, and activities of our frantic lifestyle, and engaging the mind in a thoughtful reflection on God. Waiting, to most of us, has negative connotations. It is synonymous with wasted time. To wait means not to rush or to be in a hurry. We spend the greater part of our waking hours rushing and being in a hurry.

How does our culture affect our worship? We try to rush into worship. Worship by its very nature demands preparation of heart. It involves waiting. It involves refocusing the mind and heart *from* self, others, and the details of life *to* God. When we evaluate our frame of mind and our mental and spiritual condition as we walk into the sanctuary on Sunday morning, we must admit that we rarely are prepared to meet with God and to give Him anything. Physically we are quiet but our minds are still racing and occupied with what went on before the service. Even after we mentally adjust to the quieter atmosphere, we seldom focus on God. Our attention usually fixes on the details of the service itself. We read with interest or noninterest the "news" in the bulletin. We note that the choir is "on" or "off" today. We look around to see who is there. We fight drowsiness, stand up and sit down several times, fill out an assortment of cards, and settle down to listen to the sermon, the main act. We try to follow the outline and listen eagerly for the words, "Let's all stand for the benediction." Those words signal the end. We look approvingly or disapprovingly at our watches, depending on how much after noon it is. We walk out, greet a few people, get into the car, and on the way home discuss the merits or demerits of the sermon.

How tragic! We have gone, have been sung to, preached at, and informed about coming events, but have not worshiped, because God did not receive anything from us. We were in a hurry. We were not prepared. We evaluate the experience by how much we received. We use the wrong standard to measure the impact of the exercise. To a great degree, our culture has dictated our response to God, and as it does, we are cheated of that which is fundamental to the Christian experience.

Imbalance

A second reason that worship is often sterile is that we do not balance the intellectual, emotional, and volitional expressions of worship. Man is made up of intellect, emotions, and will. His response to God must involve all three components.

Worship includes an intellectual response. Worship involves knowledge. We must know *about* God: who He is, what He has done in history, the cosmic dimensions of His plan. We must have a broad doctrinal base from which to worship because to ascribe worth to someone is to know that person. Unfortunately, we often concentrate on an intellectual response. This is important, but it is not the whole of worship. We have intellectualized the gospel to our detriment. Worship is not merely an academic exercise. We can know all the facts, repeat the correct words, and give all the right answers on cue, but intellectual involvement is not sufficient for a genuine worship experience.

We are also to respond to God emotionally. Emotional excesses in some quarters have made many of us wary of any emotional expression; yet emotions are as valid a part of our human makeup as intellect is. God created us to be emotional people. Genuine worship touches us deeply. Focusing on the greatness, power, and majesty of God creates a holy joy, an exuberance, and a liveliness which is the exact opposite of the dead, ritualistic content of much of modern worship. We are celebrating together, on the first day of the week, the resurrection of our Lord. He is alive and therefore we are alive as well. The angel's message to the shepherds attending the birth of our Lord was, "... good news of great joy ..." (Luke 2:10). Worship is a joyful, positive expression. We are not speaking about human manipulation geared to "work us up," but the genuine welling up of joy as each of us focuses on who Christ is and as we express our love for Him. Emotion is a large and valid part of any human relationship, especially interfamily relationships. We feel deeply about our relationships to our families. How much more should we feel deeply about our relationship to God, the privilege of being His child, the wonder of the cross, and the depth of His love for us.

Why is worship so often associated with deadness, sadness, and other negative impressions? It is because the trappings of worship (the liturgy, the order, the creeds, and the anthems) minus the genuine, heartfelt joy of celebration equals dead form, ritual, and mechanics. This is what Paul calls having "a form of godliness but denying its power" (II Tim. 3:5).

Not only does worship involve an intellectual and an emotional response to God, but it also must involve a volitional response. This is a constant submission to His will, a joyful, voluntary placing of oneself under His lordship and headship. True worship will involve practical decisions about ridding oneself of sin and disobedience. Part of the emotional response relates to the cleansing involved in the volitional response. David's experience of penitence and cleansing in Psalm 51 indicates this. He seems genuinely relieved at being right with God again. He prays, "Let me hear joy and gladness ..." (v. 8), "Restore to me the joy of your salvation ..." (v. 12), and after confession, "... and my tongue will sing of your righteousness" (v. 14). His decision to confess his sin produced in him an emotional relief. Tears may have been in his eyes as he prayed.

Genuine worship entails balancing these responses. The intellectual response minus the emotional and volitional responses equals deadness. It creates an academic approach to God. The emotional response minus the intellectual and volitional responses equals feelings for feelings' sake, void of a meaningful tie to the gospel's content. This leads to excess. If the volitional response is emphasized more than the other two, the result will be an unhealthy introspection and feeling of perpetual guilt. It will be characterized by repeated invitations and pressure to "decide."

Lack of Private Worship

The third reason that our corporate worship is often more form than reality is the lack of any meaningful private worship. If we are not thankful, praising, worshiping people in our private relationships to God, probably we will not engage in meaningful corporate worship. The New Testament stresses thankfulness as a characteristic of a Christian lifestyle. We are repeatedly admonished to "be thankful" and to "give thanks." Our whole relationship to God is to be characterized by the attitude and practice of thanksgiving. This quality ranks so high on the Christian's priority list because thankfulness is the antidote to diseases such as slander or bitterness. In the Psalms, David gives us a model of a beautiful relationship to God. The Psalms primarily comprise a book of worship. When we read the Psalms, we are allowed to eavesdrop on David's relationship to God, and we hear him constantly giving praise, adoration, and thanks to God, even in the midst of the most unpleasant circumstances. Paul gives us a New Testament model of the same spirit.

A helpful way to remember the components of worship is an acrostic of the word *presence*. Indeed, worshiping God is cultivating an enjoyment of His presence.

Praise God continually
Rejoice in negative circumstances
Experience God, even during trials
Seek the Lord
Expect the miraculous
Need the Lord
Confess your sins immediately
Enjoy the Lord

Christians everywhere need to develop the kind of continuous and expectant focus on God that this acrostic represents. This attitude is the basis for corporate worship. Our hearts need to be prepared, warm, and open to the Lord as we come to Him together with others. It is impossible to instantly experience fellowship with God at precisely 11:00 A.M. Corporate worship is a continuation of what has already happened, during the week, in our hearts.

Ingredients of True Worship

Two ingredients will be present in both private and corporate worship. Those ingredients are the Word of God (the Bible) and music. Both are mentioned in Colossians 3:16 and in parallel passages such as Ephesians 5:19, when Paul describes worship. Colossians 3:16 tells us to permit the Word of Christ to "dwell in you richly. ..." Worship always includes a reflective focus on the Word. The preaching and teaching of the Word in the corporate setting provides this focus. Preaching should not simply provide information, but also should hone our awareness of the greatness of our God and thus lift our spirits to Him. How many of us have had someone read to us a portion of a letter from a mutual loved one? We cherish every word! To know personally and intimately the author of the Bible is to cherish every one of His words as God's servants read and explain those words. We sometimes think of preaching as benefiting us by feeding us. It does that, for the "milk" of the Word (I Peter 2:2) is the main agent for growth in our lives. Effective preaching also stimulates worship, because it provokes response to God and focuses the mind and heart on Him.

Music is the second major ingredient of worship. The Epistles repeatedly indicate that song plays a large part in both private and corporate worship. Song is to have a teaching and admonishing ministry as we sing to "one another" (Col. 3:16). Music also serves to lift our hearts to God as we pray in song with thankfulness to Him. Ephesians 5:19 echoes the same idea; this passage is set in the context of being "filled with the Spirit." To be filled with the Spirit is to be filled with the Word of Christ and also to be filled with singing. You can gauge the clarity of your focus on God by how much your thoughts center in His Word and by how much you find yourself singing. The Psalms of David show an emphasis on these twin elements, as do the Epistles of the New Testament. Psalm 100:2 tells us to "come before him with joyful singing" and in Psalm 119 we have the classic chapter in which virtually every verse declares that David's heart is set on God's law or God's Word.

A thorough knowledge of Scripture, especially verses and passages that describe the attributes of God, is one way to cultivate a worshipful attitude. Hymns and choruses that are based on Scripture combine the Word and music, and aid worship. Christians should learn those songs. We are to worship God in "spirit and truth" (John 4:24). The Word is the truth. Singing to the Lord lifts the spirit to Him. The heart sings to the Lord. He is the audience. We must establish the habit of singing and repeating Scripture as the first and last conscious activity of the day. We thus begin and end the day in worship. Worship makes us concentrate on God for the day. Nothing will so prepare our hearts for worship as to sing Scripture to the Lord. It takes repeated effort to establish this pattern of activity, but accomplishing this will pay eternal dividends. We must see that these ingredients, in tandem, are vital to worship. Part of the problem with so many of our "quiet times" early in the morning is that they focus on the Word, but do not include any singing to the Lord. Singing warms our spirits, lifts our spirits to God, begins the communication process, and prepares us to meet with God. Look through any church hymnal and observe how many hymns are not only *about* God, but are also directed *to* God. These hymns are prayers. The Psalms include many prayers, and they were sung to God.

Once established, these patterns will carry over to the corporate celebration. Before the service, repeat Scripture verses and sing a favorite scriptural chorus or hymn to the Lord. Remember that He is the audience. We are here to give Him something. Do not categorize the choir or special music as entertainment, but as a God-given aid to lift your own heart to God. Concentrate on the words of the anthems and hymns. Make them your *personal* expressions of praise and worship. Repeat prayers, creeds, or responses to God. Many Christians are bored by liturgies, repetitions, and other formal elements of corporate worship. We are not advocating a formal style of worship, but are recognizing that liturgies aid corporate praise and expression of God's worth. Styles of worship will vary from congregation to congregation, but the purpose is the same. When we concentrate on the purpose of worship, we will realize the ingredients in the worship service are attempts to help us disengage our minds from our frantic schedules and to engage them in reflection on God.

Certainly worship is not a dead experience. Jesus came to *life* again on this day. We are celebrating His aliveness; and our singing, praying, repeating, and responding will be joyful, exuberant, and full of vitality because He lives. To focus on Him is to be fully alive. Our worship will reflect His aliveness.

Worship and Church Growth

A vibrant celebration will influence the quantitative growth of the church. We were created to be worshiping beings. A church that offers genuine worship will draw people. Such a church pulsates with the life of its head—and Jesus' life is attractive. Jesus attracts people, and a body of His children who truly celebrate His life and worth will be incredibly attractive to people. It amazes us that people accuse the church of deadness. Celebration is important not only because of its magnetic power, but also because it is usually the entry point to the fuller life of the church. Visitors will normally come to worship services first. If the experience is not attractive to them, they probably will not come to your home Bible class or Sunday school. Usually a church will not grow quantitatively if the worship service is uninviting. If this is true, failure to expend time, effort, and money to make worship an attractive part of the life of the church will guarantee quantitative status quo.

Celebration also has an impact on the church's qualitative growth. Corporate worship, more than anything else, determines the climate or atmosphere in which qualitative growth takes place. This is the only time when all of the smaller groups in the church meet. Worship demonstrates unity and love. To genuinely meet with God is to have our attitudes toward brothers and sisters in Christ positively affected. It is difficult to slander a brother after worshiping with him.

Worship provides a fullness and a wholeness to the body of Christ. We are many different identity and interest groups, but weekly corporate celebration brings all of our diversity together in joyous unity. We are a whole body. Celebration demonstrates and magnifies our wholeness. Also, since the Word of God is central to true worship and the primary means of growth (I Peter 2:2), the Holy Spirit will use the preaching and teaching of the Word to guide us into all the truth concerning Jesus and to provoke a rational, reflective response to Him. The Spirit will also use the Word to convict of sin and wrong and thus provoke a volitional confession and response to His lordship. More intangible perhaps, but also important to qualitative growth, is the climate of excitement that true celebration generates.

God. wants our worship more than anything else. The corporate expression of worship is central to the church's purpose. Worship is an inviolate spiritual principle. A dying church will not be a worshiping church. A divided church will not be a worshiping church. Worship is so critical to church health that our congregations need to be taught what worship is — its purpose, function, and place in the life of the body. A church can plan and not grow. It can program and not grow. But it will never truly worship and stay the same.

Action Items

Rate your life according to each of the principles listed in the acrostic of the word *presence*. Use a scale of 1–10, with 10 as the maximum.

> Praise God continually
> Rejoice in negative circumstances
> Experience God, even during trials
> Seek the Lord
> Expect the miraculous
> Need the Lord
> Confess your sins immediately
> Enjoy the Lord

Practice the principles in this acrostic. For one week, meditate four times daily—in the morning, at lunch, at dinner, and before going to bed—about these principles.

Rate your church and how it uses preaching, singing, and other essential qualities of worship. What can you do to help your church improve its use of these components of worship?

Bibliography

Brother Lawrence. *Practicing the Presence of God.* Edited and paraphrased by Donald E. Demaray. Grand Rapids: Baker, 1975.

Jenson, Ronald. *How to Succeed the Biblical Way.* Wheaton, IL: Tyndale, 1981. See pp. 73– 80 for more about the acrostic *presence*.

Ortlund, Anne. *Up with Worship.* Glendale, CA: Regal, 1975.

Ortlund, Raymond C. *Lord, Make My Life a Miracle.* Glendale, CA: Regal, 1974.

Wagner, C. Peter. *Your Church Can Grow.* Glendale, CA: Regal, 1976. See especially pp. 97– 109.

3

Purpose

U nderstanding the principle of purpose leads to understanding the dynamics of church growth. To understand the purpose of the church is to see clearly the product of what the church does. If our purpose is unclear and the ultimate objective is blurred, then the processes will be equally vague.

The purpose of the church is inseparably related to the purpose for the coming of Jesus Christ. We cannot consider one without considering the other. The church is God's ingenious plan for carrying the effects of Christ's work to their conclusion in time and eternity.

Purpose for Christ's Coming

Jesus' purpose in coming to earth was twofold. These two aspects are distinct but at the same time inseparable. The second is impossible without the first, and fulfillment of the first is incomplete without the second.

The first aspect of Christ's coming was redemptive. Jesus Himself gave several clear, concise statements relating to this aspect of His purpose.

43

For the Son of Man has come to seek and to save that which was lost. (Luke 19:10)

Just as the Son of Man did not come to be served, but to serve, and to give His life a ransom for many. (Matt. 20:28)

For I have not come to call the righteous, but sinners. (Matt. 9:13)

These and many other passages tell us that Jesus came to change man's relationship to God. These passages are purpose statements. They explain that a reconciliation between a holy God and sinful man was necessary. Due to the natures of God (holy) and man (sinful), a state of war existed and no peace was possible. Jesus' death on the cross provided an end to hostilities and made genuine peace between the parties. This is fundamental to understanding His purpose.

The second aspect of Christ's purpose follows from the first. This is the creative aspect. It has to do with the future of those redeemed. God's ultimate purpose is the restoration of all things, even the universe, to a state of perfect union with Himself and perfect harmony with His plan. His redemptive work is fundamental and central to this work of cosmic and personal reconciliation to Himself. In Romans 8, I Corinthians 15:17– 21, and Ephesians 1:10, we read about the comprehensive and ultimate reconciliation of all things in Christ, which is made possible by His redemptive work.

If God's ultimate purpose is to create a new cosmic order, how is this creative purpose expressed in time? Does it operate now in the lives of the redeemed? It certainly does, and in two ways.

God is first of all interested in making a new person of the redeemed sinner. God receives maximum glory only as the pardoned sinner is progressively drawn into Christ-likeness (II Cor. 5:17).

God also is interested in drawing these new people into a new community or family of redeemed ones. The relationship of the believer is not only to God (vertical), but also to one another (horizontal). Ephesians 2:11– 22 beautifully explains that, on the basis of God's redemptive work in Christ, He is drawing Jews and Gentiles into a new and radically different body, the body of Christ.

Purpose of the Church

This twofold purpose for the coming of Christ leads us to the purpose of the church. This purpose is clearly stated for us in Matthew 28:18– 20, the passage that we know as the Great Commission of our Lord. It is an awesome passage of Scripture because of the scope of the command.

The imperative (the actual command) in the passage is to "make disciples." This command is linked to the ultimate purpose of God, which is to make us different people. There are three supporting participles in the passage—go, baptize, and teach. These three activities describe the process by which disciples are made. The command to go alludes to preconversion evangelistic activity on the part of the disciples. New birth must occur before a person can become a disciple, because birth always precedes growth. Baptizing and teaching describe postconversion activities.

In this passage, Jesus is presenting, in broad strokes, the purpose and mission of the church. The Epistles and the Book of Acts spell out the role of the church in fulfilling His purpose. The mission is to the world. The problem is clear—how will the whole world come to know and feel the impact of Christ's redemptive and creative acts? The gospel message has to be extended to the whole world. How will this incredible task be performed? The answer is clear from this passage. It will occur through a multiplication process. This small group of men (disciples) will go, baptize, and teach other people, who then become disciples. These disciples will in turn make other disciples, who will make others. This will continue until Jesus comes again. This process, initiated by Jesus Himself, will guarantee that the gospel is preached to every generation, until the second coming. Spreading the gospel cannot happen any other way.

At this point we should define the word *disciple*. If the church is to make disciples, we need to know what a disciple is.

Technically, a disciple is a follower or learner. He follows a teacher for the purpose of learning. In Jesus' day, disciples attached themselves to rabbis for instruction and training. Those who attached themselves to Jesus displayed varying degrees of commitment to Him. Some were simply curious, displaying a shallow commitment. Others who followed Him evidenced deeper commitment but, during distress, deserted Him (John 6). In these cases those involved were called disciples, and technically they were. They, however, did not evidence the depth of commitment that Jesus demanded of a true disciple. He made it clear that those who would follow Him were to be characterized by a radical commitment to Him (Luke 9:24). Theirs was to be more than a teacher/student relationship. It was a relationship which would result in the student becoming like his teacher (Luke 6:40). It would result in the student sharing the teacher's commitment (to the world), His vision, and His heart. From the passages about the requirements and duties of discipleship it is clear that to be a disciple of Jesus in the truest sense of the word involves a commitment to Him which will result in becoming like Him in behavior and character. When Jesus met with His disciples in the upper room, He further defined and explained this commitment. In John 15– 16 He told them that to follow Him would mean sharing in His mission to the world and in His rejection by the world.

The Epistles further clarify the definition of a disciple. Although the word *disciple* does not occur in the Epistles, they do amplify the concept of discipleship which Jesus had explained in the Gospels.

In Colossians 1:13 Paul explains that when we receive Christ a transfer occurs. We are from the time of our birth spiritual residents of the old domain of darkness. But when we come to faith in Christ we are transferred into a new kingdom, the kingdom of God's dear Son. We change spheres of spiritual life. The practical sections of the Epistles describe for us in detail the behavior and character traits which were appropriate when we lived in the old domain of darkness (Col. 3:5– 17; Eph. 4:32). In these passages and many others we are repeatedly admonished to "put off" certain behavior and to "put on" other behavior. The Holy Spirit is to produce in us a new kind of character, described as "fruit" of the Spirit (Gal. 5:22– 23). These nine characteristics describe the life of Jesus Christ. The Holy Spirit is committed to reproducing in us the life of Christ. This is what Jesus meant in John 15 when He explained the "abiding" life. Union with Christ results in a new kind and quality of life, described as fruit. This lifestyle glorifies God (15:1– 8) and includes personal and corporate witness to the person of Christ (15:26). This new kind of life extends to succeeding generations of disciples.

From the Gospels, the Book of Acts, and the Epistles, it is clear that a disciple is one who is progressively developing, in his behavior and character, into the likeness of Jesus Christ and who is committed to reproducing that life and likeness in others, through the exercise of his spiritual gift. This is the commission of Matthew 28:18– 20.

How the Church Fulfills Its Purpose

If making new people is God's plan for extending the gospel into the whole world, where does the church fit in? The Book of Acts and the Epistles answer this question.

As the gospel was extended to the first-century world, the resulting disciples clustered together in localized bodies called churches. These groups of "called-out" ones (*ekklesia*) fashioned themselves after the Jewish synagogues but with some important new goals and motivations.

These local churches, in God's plan, were instruments to perfect, mature, train, and develop the disciples into the likeness of Christ. These local assemblies of disciples had two basic functions.

The Church Edifies

The local church makes disciples (edifies). The church is God's creative way of developing new men. Every program and activity in the church aims at this ultimate objective. As men and women come into the church (transfer) from the old kingdom of darkness, they carry with them old behavior, habits, thought processes, and character traits. They need to be discipled (i.e., changed into new people with new behavior, habits, and thoughts). The church is God's agent to accomplish this objective. The church edifies believers in four ways.

Gifted men

The first way the church accomplishes its purpose is by providing gifted men to equip the disciples. Ephesians 4:11–12 tells us that pastors/teachers have been given to the church with the specific job of "equipping" (v. 12, NASB) people for service. The passage goes on to define the pastor's work. It means more than fitting a person for a specific functional task. It involves leading the body into spiritual maturity, stability, and fullness (vv. 13–15). The church is to disciple its members—to develop them into Christ-likeness. The pastor/teacher is given to the church of God to lead the body into "the *fulness of Christ*" (v. 13, NASB, italics ours). He has twin functions which allow him to accomplish this task. The words *pastor* and *teacher* describe these functions. These functions are combined in one office, separate but inseparable. One is the teaching function: the ministry of the Word. The Word of God, according to I Peter 2:2, is the agent of spiritual growth. It is the primary means through which change occurs in the transferred disciple. The pastor/teacher unfolds, in public and private, the meaning of the Word. The second function is a pastoral or shepherding one. It refers to the responsibility of total care. The needs of the disciple go beyond the need for teaching. He has other needs— acceptance, a feeling of worth, love—that the church, as God's family, is to meet. Because the church is a family, it provides a loving, supportive structure in which the disciple grows into Christ-likeness. The pastor leads by example and in the development of a caring, shepherding structure in which the disciple grows to maturity.

Varied activities

The second way in which the church develops disciples is by providing a variety of activities. This refers to the programming function of the church. In Acts 2:42 we read about some of the activities in which the disciples were involved. Those activities included teaching, prayer, fellowship, and breaking of bread. We are not told specifically what programming structures the early church developed. We do not know all the different ways that fellowship took place or prayer occurred, but we do know that the church was involved in activities which met existing needs.

The body of Christ is made up of people with divergent needs. Believers are of varied ages, maturity, and backgrounds. Programming is an attempt to meet these needs. A high-school student has different needs than a middle-aged single parent does, but both are found in the same body and both need to be taught and shepherded. Many people misunderstand programming. Programming is perceived as unspiritual. The problem is that much of the church's programming has lost its discipling focus. We have some activities in which we participate merely because we have always done so. They are dead and maintain the status quo. Actually, programming, with the proper purpose, is for people. It meets people's needs. A church's social activities, its Bible studies, or its activities for different age groups contribute to the making of new men. If an activity does not contribute to this objective, it should be evaluated and either changed or discontinued.

Climate for growth

A third way the church makes disciples is by providing a certain climate or atmosphere in which the Holy Spirit can mature a person at his own rate. Climate, to a great extent, determines the growth of any living thing. Since the church is a living organism, climate determines its growth. Two things are important to note about the climate in which disciples are made. First, the Holy Spirit is responsible for maturing the new disciple. Philippians 1:6 tells us that "he who began a good work in you will carry it on to completion until the day of Christ Jesus." The second thing to remember about climate is that the Holy Spirit has a different timetable for each disciple. Everyone does not grow at the same rate. Everyone in the church is at a different stage of growth and development. This is probably the most overlooked factor in church growth. It makes church growth complex. Climate refers to the loving, caring, nonjudgmental attitude that allows individuals the freedom to grow according to the Holy Spirit's timetable for them. It is the lack of pressure to perform or to conform to someone else's standards or schedule. The requirements of the Word and the commitments of discipleship are made clear, but the Holy Spirit is free to work as He chooses.

Staid separatism, legalism, deadness, divisiveness, and any number of other diseases often characterize a church. These cause a restrictive and unfavorable climate.

Exercise of gifts

The fourth way that the church makes disciples is by structuring its ministry around the exercise of gifts and the uniqueness of each member. Growth into Christ-likeness will occur as the disciple is taught, but also as he learns to use his spiritual gift to minister to the body. He must be involved in meaningful ministry. In our church, we emphasize that every person should be involved in at least one ministry. Involvement benefits the church, and allows individuals to grow spiritually. Each person must learn to serve and give as well as to take. Involvement in ministry provides the balance needed to grow at the maximum rate. Involvement must be tailored to maturity. A believer's first ministry may be ushering or nursery care, but whatever it is, it will let that person demonstrate ability and faithfulness and will provide opportunity to serve and build up the whole body.

The Church Evangelizes

Not only does the church make disciples, but it also ministers to (evangelizes) those still in the old kingdom of darkness. This second function provides balance to its purpose. A church seeking to make disciples — without an emphasis on outreach to the larger community — runs the risk of becoming ingrown, selfish, and negative.

When we speak of the church as a base of ministry to the community, we are not speaking of a door-to-door canvass. We are speaking of the magnetic quality of the life of a body of people. Since lives are being transformed by what is happening in the church, those still in the old kingdom will be attracted like a magnet by two things.

Unbelievers will be attracted first by the observable reality of the disciple's behavior and character change (I Peter 3:15). The greatest apologetic in the world is a person, living and working among those still in darkness, who is changing and becoming a new person. Jesus is attractive. If Christians are becoming more and more like Jesus, they should be attracting people to Him. The spiritually dead are attracted to life. The contrast between a spiritually dead person and a spiritually alive person is dramatic and noticeable. People should be able to see the difference in the way the new disciple handles problems, pressures, and trial. Evangelism is much more of an audio-visual process than we know. Jesus intended it to be so. People need to see as well as hear. Optimum evangelistic results will occur when there is a simultaneous opportunity for both.

The second attraction to those still in the old kingdom will be the observable reality of the loving relationships between the disciples (John 13:35). This is true because the relationships in the old kingdom are so often false, shallow, and short-term. When the non-Christian sees genuine love expressed among members of the body, it makes an immediate impression and has a magnetic attraction. All of us thirst for genuine relationships. This is why much of the evangelistic activity in our church is done in groups (e.g., evangelistic events such as breakfasts or luncheons at someone's home). We want non-Christians to see the fellowship of Christian groups as often as possible. Often, after these occasions, the non-Christian will say that he or she has never seen people like this or felt this kind of love and acceptance. Thus we provide an opportunity to see as well as hear the message.

Extending the gospel message involves not only telling non-Christians some theological facts, but also demonstrating before them changed lives and healed relationships. Becoming a Christian will usually involve not only hearing the gospel but also observing it in action.

The church sends radically changed people into the old kingdom of alienated, hurting, lost people. This intentional, visible contrast between the old and new is the basis for evangelism.

How Disciplemaking Affects Growth

Rallying the members of a local church around the common objective of making disciples will have enormous implications for the growth of the church. Many churches have lost sight of their purpose. Knowing and understanding the objective gives direction and meaning to all that a church does.

An awareness that outreach to the community and the world is central to its very existence affects a church's quantitative growth. When a church sees itself as a base of ministry to those living around it, it will be continually praying and thinking about effective ways to witness to the community. This will be a natural preoccupation because the church exists to minister.

Qualitatively, teaching, preaching, and ministry will be influenced by knowing what our ultimate objective is. To see ourselves involved in producing new people and a new community of people is exciting. To make a permanent, eternal impact on lives is the highest priority of life. All of our workers in every ministry need to see that they contribute to making new men. These new men will then introduce others to the means for becoming new men. The process never stops.

Organic development is also affected. Church leaders need to see the results of their labor. These results will challenge Christians to attain greater effectiveness and to seek converts. Many people in the church work in functional, behind-the-scenes jobs. Nonetheless, they contribute to the product—new men.

One of the most worthwhile projects that a pastor and his leadership can do is to develop a purpose statement—a clear, concise statement of why the church exists. This statement should be spoken about, prayed about, printed, and ingrained in the consciousness of the people. Does the church membership understand why the church exists? A good purpose statement is crucial in helping everyone understand the church's role. The pastor and leaders need to:

1. See it clearly (single-minded direction)
2. Want it desperately (deep-seated desire)
3. Accomplish it enthusiastically (God-given enthusiasm)
4. Follow it faithfully (bulldogged tenacity)
5. Review, realign, and rededicate themselves regularly (regular evaluation)

The church will have a direction, an exciting climate, and an over-riding sense of mission in proportion to the membership's awareness of the church's purpose.

Action Items

Using the guidelines listed at the end of this chapter, evaluate your church's sense of purpose.

Write a purpose statement for your church. A purpose statement should encompass the comprehensive, long-range reason(s) why your church should continue to exist.

When you write this purpose statement, explain, in simple, direct sentences, why your church exists today. For example, you should:

> answer basic questions, such as why your church conducts worship services or youth programs, or what your church should be as part of the body of Christ;
>
> make sure your purpose statement deals with the vertical relationship between your church and God;
>
> concentrate on why your church exists, rather than discussing specific programs, since we will concentrate on programs in a subsequent chapter;
>
> strive for quality and honesty, rather than attempting to write a perfect purpose statement.

Evaluate how effective you, your church leaders, and your congregation are in the following areas.

P=Poor
O=Outstanding

	You	Leadership	Church
Single-minded direction	P 1 2 3 4 5 O	P 1 2 3 4 5 O	P 1 2 3 4 5 O
Deep-seated desire	P 1 2 3 4 5 O	P 1 2 3 4 5 O	P 1 2 3 4 5 O
God-given enthusiasm	P 1 2 3 4 5 O	P 1 2 3 4 5 O	P 1 2 3 4 5 O
Bulldogged tenacity	P 1 2 3 4 5 O	P 1 2 3 4 5 O	P 1 2 3 4 5 O
Regular evaluation	P 1 2 3 4 5 O	P 1 2 3 4 5 O	P 1 2 3 4 5 O

God can build all of these qualities into your life and sharpen your effectiveness as a spiritual leader. Decide which of these characteristics you particularly desire and need to develop. Circle it on the list above. Then consider the following questions and complete the exercises.

1. What is the opposite of this characteristic?

2. How does its opposite manifest itself in your life? Be specific.

3. The opposite may well represent sin. If so, confess it, repent, and accept God's forgiveness.

4. Express to God your desire to manifest the new characteristic.

5. Make a list of all the ways your life this week (e.g., habits, words, actions, or schedule) would be different if you possessed this characteristic. Be specific.

6. Rely on the power of the indwelling, resurrected Christ to help you *live* this way in the next week. As these changes occur, make a note of them as a reminder to praise Him.

Suggest three things you could do to help your pastor or a church leader to develop these characteristics in his life.

Bibliography

Charles E. Fuller Institute of Evangelism and Church Growth, Box 989, Pasadena, CA 91102. The institute has materials that give guidelines for writing purpose statements.

DeMoss, Arthur, and Enlow, David. *How to Change Your World in 12 Weeks.* Old Tappan, NJ: Revell, 1977.

Getz, Gene A. *Sharpening the Focus of the Church.* Chicago: Moody, 1976.

Jenson, Ronald. *How to Succeed the Biblical Way.* Wheaton, IL: Tyndale, 1981. See pp. 109–116 for more information about the five factors involved in writing a purpose statement.

MacArthur, John, Jr. *The Church: The Body of Christ.* Grand Rapids: Zondervan, 1973.

Schaller, Lyle E. *Parish Planning.* Nashville: Abingdon, 1971.

Schuller, Robert H. *Move Ahead with Possibility Thinking.* Paperback edition. Old Tappan, NJ: Revell, 1973.

4

Diagnosis

In an earlier chapter, we said that church growth depends on health. All living things grow unless disease impedes growth. We assume an organism will grow if it stays healthy. Since the church is a living organism, it will naturally and spontaneously grow if it stays healthy.

Maintaining physical health depends on diagnosis. To diagnose is to evaluate and analyze vital signs and body function and thus determine the state of health. Diagnosis can be preventative—for instance, the annual checkup when nothing is known to be wrong. Diagnosis can also be the response to a symptom of something known to be wrong. As an example, I may have a high fever but not know what the problem is. The fever is a symptom of an unknown malady. I go to the doctor for diagnosis. He will determine what the problem is, and then recommend treatment.

Diagnosis is a much-neglected principle of church growth. It corresponds to the process by which physical health is maintained. It may be preventative (spotting potential problems before they develop into serious illness) or it may be the effort to pinpoint disease when several symptoms are already present. In either case it involves evaluating and analyzing a church ministry, with the objective of maintaining health.

Many churches exist in a state of perpetual ill health because no one has diagnosed the churches' diseases. A sense that "something is wrong" or "we need to do something" is a symptom of illness which needs to be pinpointed and corrected before the church deteriorates further and the disease becomes terminal. Paul instructed Timothy to "watch your life and your doctrine closely" (I Tim. 4:16). In effect, Paul told Timothy to practice regular diagnosis and to monitor the effectiveness of his ministry. This personal exhortation also applies to the church.

The Basis for Diagnosis

We need to consider the basis for effective diagnosis. The techniques of medical diagnosis give us a clue. How does the doctor diagnose the cause of my high fever? He does not feel my forehead and render immediate judgment. He first performs a series of data-gathering exercises, using various instruments and methods. He gathers data with an occasional grunt, wince, frown, or smile. After he knows the facts, he will render a judgment about my condition.

We must also collect data if we intend to diagnose a church's ailments. We need facts with which to work. Different people may reach different conclusions about what the facts prove, but facts give an objective basis for discussion and decision. Many church decisions are based on subjective opinion and inadequate data.

Churches can obtain accurate, pertinent data in several ways. Churches need good records about attendance, membership, and giving. These records not only tell us what we have done, but also give us a basis for projection and planning. Surveys of congregational attitudes and needs are also useful data-gathering tools.[1] Sometimes church leaders become separated from the people and make decisions on the basis of a few opinions, or on what they suppose members think.

Two years ago, in conjunction with a church-growth consultant, our church took a congregational survey in which we asked several questions about membership, giving, and involvement in the life and min-

1. Several books give practical advice about using questionnaires, graphs, and other methods of gathering and interpreting data. See Virgil Gerber, *God's Way to Keep a Church Going and Growing* (Glendale, CA: Regal, 1974); Lloyd Perry, *Getting The Church on Target* (Chicago: Moody, 1977); and Waldo J. Werning, *Vision and Strategy for Church Growth* (Chicago: Moody, 1977).

istry of the church. We separated the surveys according to whether the respondents were members or nonmembers, tallied all the answers, and plotted the results on a graph. The results of that simple exercise were astounding. For the first time many of our suspicions were confirmed as facts. For example, the survey confirmed that many people who regularly attended our church waited a long time before joining. The survey also confirmed that members gave more, were more involved, and participated in church activities more than nonmembers did. We concluded that we needed a regular, structured emphasis on membership. The result was a new-member orientation series and a greatly enlarged membership. This is an example of basing program decisions on adequate data. We sensed that all those things were true, but we did not act until the facts confirmed our guesses.

Leaders need to know the reality of their situation before they can make changes. Only good data can provide this basis for diagnosis.

Before we can discuss the process of diagnosis, we must understand what health is. When we talk about physical health, we understand that health implies not only the absence of disease, but also that each part of the body functions properly, both by itself and in relation to the other parts. Diagnosis begins with an awareness of the diseases that can attack an organism. In making a diagnosis, one must discern the difference between a disease and its symptoms. A symptom is an outward, visible effect of a disease.

These principles also apply to the church. In terms of the church, "disease" means that it deviates from biblical patterns and standards for its life. Often we have a hazy concept about what constitutes a healthy church. But the New Testament outlines the standards against which we must measure our church life. When a church does not measure up to those biblical standards, the church is diseased.

We should differentiate between disease and certain sociological phenomena which can restrict the growth of a church. Peter Wagner's term *sociological strangulation* describes a condition in which a church's growth is restricted by lack of services such as adequate facilities, staff, or parking (*Your Church Can Grow*, pp. 124– 146). This condition is not a disease, because a church may be healthy in terms of its purpose, vision, and programming, and still lack these services. The same thing may be true of churches which find themselves in changing neighborhoods. This does not imply sickness, although if a church does not deal with these problems, it may eventually have to close its doors.

Diseases Within the Church

Several diseases afflict churches. Church leaders must diagnose the symptoms, pinpoint specific problems, and take prayerful action to treat the disease. We will mention five diseases that affect churches.

Toleration of Known Sin

The first disease that saps the life from a church is the toleration of known sin. Virtually every page of the Epistles includes a list of unacceptable behavior and character traits. Many of these relate to how we use words. These sins are deadly and have a cancerous effect in the cells which make up the church. The Epistles consistently mention—and discourage—the sins of gossip, slander, evil report, and others. These actions will destroy unity, and the unity of a diverse body of people is the quality which, more than any other, draws people to Christ and the church. Many other things are expressly forbidden in the New Testament—for instance, moral laxity or an unforgiving spirit. The New Testament gives us clear guidelines about how to deal with these things. Words such as *rebuke, exhort,* and *admonish* are all used in the context of ministering to "one another." Procedures for church discipline are given to us in Matthew 18 and I Corinthians 5 and 6. Although the commands are clear and the procedures for dealing with sin are explicit, we rarely deal with sin unless it is blatant.

The symptoms of this disease include lack of growth, division, negative attitudes, a climate not conducive to growth, and disunity in the body.

Lack of Desire to Grow

A second disease is the lack of a desire to grow (in the organic and qualitative senses, as well as in a quantitative sense). This clearly violates the spirit of the teachings contained in the New Testament. As long as this attitude persists, unconfessed and uncorrected, the church will deteriorate until it dies. Growth is not an option. It is natural. The church is to minister to the world around it. Jesus came for that reason (Luke 19:10). Ephesians 4 speaks repeatedly about building the body, and the growth of the body. Not to pursue the goal of reaching the maximum number of people in the most effective way is sin and constitutes an insidious sickness which, like a perpetual headache, dulls the body's sensitivity.

The symptoms of this disease will be apathy, an attitude that "life goes on as usual," and an obvious lack of growth.

Lack of Commitment to Prayer

A third common disease is the lack of a strong commitment to prayer as the foundation for all of a church's ministry. If we do not pray, we imply that we can initiate and produce spiritual results. This is to labor under deadly false assumptions. Malnutrition cuts a physical body off from its supply of life-giving nutrients. Eventually it causes death. Prayerlessness cuts us off from the only source of spiritual life. Self-effort will prove fatal.

The symptoms of this disease will include apathy, lack of a joyful, enthusiastic lifestyle, lack of sensitivity to other people and their needs, a lack of awareness about the power of God, and a "life as usual" attitude. A remedial step in dealing with all disease is a bold call to repentance and prayer.

Lack of Leadership Development

A fourth disease is the lack of both leadership development and the exercise of spiritual gifts. This characterizes a church that is trying to grow without involving its people in ministry. This is contrary to the biblical pattern of church ministry. I Corinthians 12–14, Ephesians 4:11–16, and other passages spell out the involvement of every believer in a ministry that God has equipped him to do. To minister is not an option.

The symptom of this disease is one group of people doing all the work. The average church needs to reevaluate its work force. How many people minister to the body? How many minister to the community? How many jobs does the average worker perform? How many hours does the average worker spend per week in ministry? What kinds of training are available for workers in various ministries? These questions form the basis for diagnosing this disease.

Extreme Forms of Church Government

A fifth disease is an extreme congregational form of church government. We know of a small church which has more than fifty elected positions. A congregation cannot be sufficiently informed about the people and the necessary qualifications for all of those jobs to ensure that the right people will perform the ministries. This form of church government goes against every biblical and management principle of leadership development. The issue here is qualification. For example, how many churches have elected Sunday-school leaders who are not remotely qualified to do their jobs?

The symptom of this disease is stagnation and a loss of momentum resulting from the wrong people doing a task. Since elections "lock in" personnel until the next election, the pastor and other leaders often find themselves frustrated because leaders cannot be replaced. Under this system, flexibility is missing.

Leadership development and appointment to ministry positions have to be carried out by those leaders who know the needs of the body, and the qualifications of potential personnel, and who have an overview of the total ministry.

Diagnosis begins with objectives which reflect biblical standards of church health. As church leaders begin to recognize the ingredients of a healthy church, they can diagnose symptoms and treat the disease.

The Benefits of Diagnosis

Effective diagnosis has two benefits. Diagnosis will force a church to focus on *purpose,* not on institutional maintenance. Evaluation has meaning only if we measure progress against a specific objective or goal. For instance, to say we are going to diagnose our Sunday-school program is meaningless unless we have some objectives for our Sunday school. Without clear objectives we would not know which diagnostic questions to ask. "How are we doing?" is a good question, but irrelevant unless we also ask, "with respect to what?"

Diagnosis keeps us asking the right questions about how we are fulfilling our purpose. This forces us away from merely maintaining the institution. "We do it this way because we've always done it this way" is the classic cry of many terminally ill churches. Many young pastors find themselves working around, rather than with, the governing boards of their churches, because those boards apparently want to maintain institutions which have long since lost their sense of purpose. Lack of diagnosis allows a church to settle into an institutional rut which becomes comfortable but hard to climb out of.

A second benefit of effective diagnosis is that it provides a structure for reflection. Diagnosis forces us to evaluate, ask questions, recommend change, and discuss objectives. Many church meetings reflect a preoccupation with immediate concerns. Diagnosis helps us to set long-range goals, to ask the important questions, and to look at what we are and where we are going.

The Challenge of Diagnosis

Diagnosis is a difficult process. Sometimes we are not willing to evaluate ministries, because we are afraid of offending people by evaluating their performance. In our church, we recently took a survey in our adult Sunday-school classes. We asked questions about the style and skills of the teachers, and the content of their lessons. It was difficult to discuss the results with the teachers, but necessary. Diagnosis must be done in the right spirit. It is difficult to do, especially with volunteer labor, but it is necessary if a church is to maintain high-quality programs. We have found that people appreciate pointers about increasing their effectiveness, especially if they are evaluated according to agreed-on objectives.

Another thing we wish to say about diagnosis is that leadership must take the initiative. The pastor and lay leaders must begin to take the pulse of the body—to ask questions in a structured way. They may wish to appoint a task force to study aspects of the ministry, take surveys, or perform any number of other diagnostic processes. Whatever the tool or the process, the members must sense that excellence is desired, that objectives in every ministry are essential, and that regular evaluation is a normal, natural part of maintaining a healthy body.

The Effect of Diagnosis on Growth

Effective diagnosis and evaluation will affect the growth of the church quantitatively, qualitatively, and organically.

Quantity will be affected because diagnosis allows us to isolate needs and then meet them. When needs begin to be met, people will begin to come. For example, we began a ministry for single people in our church because of the varied needs in the singles community. As the ministry began to develop, more people were attracted. As diagnosis begins to reveal needs, a church can develop programs to meet those needs. Diagnosis allows a church to maximize its time and resources. We can allocate our resources in a meaningful way if we know the needs to be met.

Diagnosis forces a church to emphasize qualitative excellence. It also forces accountability to one another. If we regularly evaluate our ministries in terms of specific objectives, it will be clear when we have failed and why. It will be acceptable to fail and learn from failure. We will not try to justify failure, but will admit when we have not achieved what we set out to do. This spirit of openness and honesty is impossible apart from regular evaluation. So many churches have no accountability and no emphasis on excellence because there are no objectives or evaluative processes. These churches never know where they are. They keep doing what they have always done.

Diagnosis affects a church's organic growth, too. The leaders will know that the church is accomplishing what it set out to do. They will have the satisfaction of knowing that needs are being met. If an area of ministry is weak (i.e., not meeting objectives) the leaders will know it, and know why. How many churches are laboring with the vague feeling that they are not going anywhere? Evaluation gives direction and a sense of right priorities.

Action Items

How is diagnosis practiced in your church? Be specific.

Of the five diseases mentioned, which affect your church?

What specific steps can you take to correct that?

Bibliography

Charles E. Fuller Institute of Evangelism and Church Growth, Box 989, Pasadena, CA 91102. Materials for diagnosing a church's health.

Engel, James F. *How Can I Get Them to Listen?* Grand Rapids: Zondervan, 1977.

_____, and Norton, H. Wilbert. *What's Gone Wrong with the Harvest?* Grand Rapids: Zondervan, 1975.

Gerber, Virgil. *Evangelism: A Manual For Church Growth.* Pasadena, CA: William Carey Library, 1973.

Griffin, Em. *The Mind Changers.* Wheaton, IL: Tyndale, 1976.

Schaller, Lyle E. *Parish Planning.* Nashville: Abingdon, 1971. See especially the section about annual audit.

5

Priorities

In developing a healthy church, leaders and members will quickly realize that they must continually evaluate programs and activities. Some activities will be considered more important than others. The former will become the church's priorities. Before church members can classify a program as a priority, they must judge that program's relative importance at a given time.

Establishing priorities is an obstacle for many churches. A church that lacks well-defined priorities — and the structure for evaluating programs — will drift from program to program, with no progress toward fulfilling its purpose.

The nature of the church requires that church members make choices about programs. There is diversity in the body of Christ. There are differences in age, spiritual maturity, and life situations. These differences represent a variety of needs and demands which cannot all be met at the same time. Determining priorities not only involves a judgment about the value or importance of an activity, but it also entails a judgment about the relative value of the activity with respect to time. Our church would like to be involved in many activities, but it cannot do all of them now. The number of possible ministries necessitates choice. Someone or some group has to determine how the needs rank in order of importance. This process of choosing demands total dependence on God and His wisdom.

Establish Priorities

Establishing priorities in any church will test the mettle of a pastor and/or leaders. It becomes the ultimate test of leadership and management skill. This is true because of the diverse nature of the body.

The process becomes complicated because there are various pressure sources. Every member becomes a potential lobbyist for any activity or ministry which he or she favors. People will have definite opinions about things which relate to their needs. Because so many needs are represented in the body, the pastor will be constantly urged to do something to meet them. There are potential ministries corresponding to every age level and situation represented in the church (e.g., singles, the elderly, college students, junior-high or high-school students). Every one of these groups is a lobby. Each wants the church to develop a ministry to meet its needs, and does not understand why the church cannot initiate that ministry.

The situation corresponds to political structure in our country. Hundreds of special-interest groups demand that something be done to meet their particular needs. For example, when former President Jimmy Carter eliminated certain water projects, Western constituents created storms of protest. Everyone has his own cause to which he automatically assigns first priority because of his deeply-felt need.

In the church, this lobbying is not done unkindly, nor is it meant to put pressure on anyone. It springs from an honest desire to meet needs. It also springs naturally from lacking an overview of the church ministry. Each group is limited in its particular scope. The pastor and a select group of leaders are the only ones with a total picture of the church's needs. Since these leaders see the total picture, they are the ones who have the responsibility of determining priorities.

Lobbying, although natural, can have two negative implications.

First, the pastor may take the pressure personally, feel a great sense of guilt, and try to meet all the needs simultaneously. If he does not work with priorities, he will overwork himself trying to respond to each pressure source, even though he does not have the leadership or financial resources to do the job.

Second, this process is potentially divisive. Many churches regularly experience tension and division at budget time because the budget, more than any other document, reflects a church's priorities. A person or group may feel deeply about the need for a particular ministry and not understand why another ministry takes priority in terms of personnel or money allocated. Jealousy, bitterness, and disunity may develop. This is why setting priorities demands the highest level of spiritual maturity. Many churches experience division when groups disagree about priorities.

Relate Priorities to Purpose

Several principles relate to setting priorities in the church. The first principle is that churches need to maintain their perspectives. Priorities must relate to purpose. It will be impossible to determine priorities without knowing our ultimate purpose. Programming is what we do to accomplish our purpose. Priorities tell us how we should program, at a specific time, to reach our objectives and to fulfill our purpose. Programming tells us what to do. Priorities give us guidelines about when to do it, while purpose tells us why we are doing it.

Let us illustrate this principle. Suppose a church decides that it needs to launch an evangelistic effort to reach young couples in the community. The church concludes this after surveying the community and realizing the church is in an area with several large apartment complexes where hundreds of young couples live. A factor in the decision is that the church has only a handful of young couples. On the basis of this diagnosis, the church decides its future lies with young couples. The church makes a programming decision and begins to devise a strategy to "reach" the people in those apartment complexes. This decision is laudable, but after a closer look at the purpose of the church, it might become obvious that the proposed evangelistic thrust is not a priority *at this time.* After more thought the leaders realize that the reason for evangelism is folding people into the fellowship of the body of Christ. Nothing in this church (at the present time) would attract a young couple. The nursery facilities are run-down and poorly staffed, there is no Sunday-school class for young couples, there is no social structure which a young couple would find attractive. In short, the barn is not ready to contain the harvest. In light of the bigger picture, improving the nursery or the young couples' Sunday-school class might be higher priorities than the evangelistic effort. The evangelistic effort is a good idea and could be initiated, but it might not be wise to launch it now.

Someone, usually the pastor and his staff, must always look at the big picture. They need to look beyond the present situation, to project months and even years ahead. Generally this is not the case. Pastors are so occupied with immediate crises that they can barely think about tomorrow, let alone five years from now. This is why setting priorities is related so closely to planning. We always need to project the *next* steps. If we do not look at long-range goals, our view of the priorities will be fuzzy. We need to ask ourselves which staff and ministries will help us to achieve our objectives in the most effective way. We must ask which ministries represent priorities. We then need to add staff and programs to attain those objectives. These are difficult choices, but we know that unless we determine priorities on the basis of our overall purpose, we will not achieve significant results and will waste precious time and money.

Do a Few Things Well

The second principle for determining priorities is that a church needs to concentrate on doing a few things well. Because of the variety of needs to be met, the temptation is to try to do everything at once. We tend to be overwhelmed by need. A pastor needs to look at his own time commitment. Since he cannot do everything well, how should he use his time? Three factors limit programming, especially in a small church. They are leadership personnel, money, and facilities. Many pastors will try to provide, in time and energy, what the church lacks in these three areas. When trying to make a programming decision we need to ask four questions:

1. Who will do this ministry and how much time will the pastor have to spend to train this person and maintain his motivation?
2. How much will the program cost?
3. What facilities are necessary, and what ones are available?
4. If the proposed ministry grows and develops, what leadership, money, and facilities will it require in one or two years?

We are not suggesting that we should discourage interested workers from beginning a ministry or that we should not move by faith, trusting

God to provide needs. We are suggesting that a church not try to do everything at once and that it concentrate on those things which it does best and which have attracted its present congregation. A church can add programs, facilities, and staff in an orderly way as God provides the resources.

For example, we know that a family is attracted to a church if it senses that all of the family members can be ministered to and that excellent programs exist to meet the needs of the whole family. A church needs to concentrate, then, on building at least one attractive ministry for each age level. In surveys that we have done within our own church, we found people initially were attracted by the quality of the preaching and teaching, and the quality of the children's ministries. Each church needs to evaluate how much it concentrates on developing five of its functions, and then determine its priorities. The order of priority will differ from church to church, depending on its strength in each area.

Worship service

The worship service includes preaching and teaching. If the preaching is mediocre and other strong, attractive ministries do not compensate for it, the church probably will not grow.

Children's ministry

One of the strong ministries in our church is the boys' and girls' club programs. The children's ministry includes an attractive and well-staffed nursery. Clubs, Sunday school, and camps are potential children's ministries. Concentrate on the nursery and on improving your best programs before you add new ones.

Youth ministries

Most churches probably will feel the need to provide full-time staff for this ministry before they do so for other programs. One of the first questions a new family will ask is, "What do you have for youth?" If your church does not have a full-time staff for youth ministries, concentrate on encouraging a team of people to develop an excellent Sunday school and a social structure for the junior-high and senior-high youth.

Adult ministries

There are scores of potential adult programs. Concentrate on developing—one at a time—good adult Sunday-school classes, small meetings in members' homes, and men's and women's Bible-study classes. Add new ones as leadership becomes available. Also concentrate on developing social activities for adults. These should preferably be in conjunction with the educational activities.

Leadership

A pastor must concentrate on strengthening the church's governing board or council. If this group is spiritually weak or has limited vision, and is making programming and priority decisions, the ability of the body to attract new members will reflect those weaknesses.

We believe that if a pastor is to be effective, he has to concentrate on a few ministries which, if strong, will attract new families to the church. We see small, struggling churches trying to establish singles ministries and specialized evangelistic campaigns while the basic ministries are still weak. Remember these specialized ministries are necessary, but maybe not now. We are not judging the importance, but the timing.

Recognize the Relationships Between Activities

The third principle in determining priorities is that we must recognize the relationships between activities. This is essential in deciding priorities. There may be no apparent relationship between adult ministries and the nursery program, but there is a connection, as we tried to point out earlier. If we want to attract young families, we need to ask what must happen in the church so this can take place. When we think about this, developing an attractive nursery program may well be our number-one priority. The same would apply to children's and youth ministries. The pastor needs to think about the relationships of all of the church's activities.

Activities are generally interdependent. If one activity is weak, another or several others might be weakened as well. In every church, structures exist to support major ministries. The behind-the-scenes committees and boards which affect the quality of these structures may be priority items if we are looking at the relationship of the activities.

Anticipate and Overcome Barriers

A pastor who is intent on convincing his church to set priorities can expect to face opposition, especially if the church has traditionally done specific things in a specific way. The body of Christ is a complex organism and determining priorities can be the most complex process within that organism. Pastors may face several obstacles as they try to establish priorities in the church.

Lack of Education

The leaders of most churches have not been trained to understand the importance of setting priorities. The concepts of purpose, objectives, priorities, and philosophy of ministry are foreign to these people. Ministries continue as they have for years. In this case, change is needed. The issue is how we communicate the need for change. Pastors need to be master educators. But the pastor must be aware of several factors.

The pastor himself needs a clear perception (overview) of what to do and why he wants the church to do this. He must know the biblical principles involved. For example, a pastor presents a proposal for establishing small groups within the church. Members of the board greet the proposal with stony silence. Why? Perhaps they were not sufficiently prepared. One way to educate the board members about the need for small groups is to do a Bible study about the "one another" ministries — loving, caring, encouraging — mentioned in the Epistles. Make the board members see the biblical basis for this ministry. Then ask, "How are we ministering to one another in this way in our church?" Involve the board members in questioning and struggling with the problem of providing this kind of life within the church. Work through the process with an open Bible, whenever possible. Do not propose a program without adequately preparing the leaders. To further illustrate this point, we will use another example. A pastor proposed a new method of outreach. The members of the governing board rejected his idea, and he could not understand why. As we talked, he realized that he had not discussed the issues — need and biblical precedent — with them.

A new pastor needs to build trust before he launches new programs or tries to change opinions that formed over the years. Change takes time. Concentrate on ministering personally and developing confidence, trust, and loyalty. All the while, lay the biblical and philosophical groundwork for change. People need to know that you are committed to helping them.

Know the power structure. Who really has the greatest influence? It will take some time to find this out but you will save time and grief if you will do it. Which of the board members, if any, thinks philosophically and biblically about issues? In every leadership group, a few people will say "yea" or "nay" and the others will follow. Find out who wields the power.

Anticipate opposition to your ideas. Neutralize it by educating people. This is crucial. Find out about feelings or prejudices before making proposals to the group. You will find that the greater the proposed change, the more groundwork you will need to do. What many pastors interpret as rebellion and stubbornness on the part of their boards is simply a lack of preparation and education.

Lack of Experience

Lack of experience relates to a lack of a model. If a pastor and his leaders have never worked within a priority-setting structure, it will be difficult to start. We learn by receiving information, but we learn best by observation. If we are starting a new ministry in our church, we always try to find where it is being done successfully elsewhere. We have visited ministries around the country. We do not copy the details, but the model is always helpful. A good question to ask is, "Where is it working?" A phone call, a visit, or printed material from a place where a ministry is working is invaluable. Leaders need to observe the principles of ministry in action.

Lack of Evaluation

Lack of evaluation refers to not understanding diagnosis and its importance in the church. Diagnosis must precede priority-setting because only diagnosis provides a clear perception of needs. In setting priorities, diagnosis tells us which ministries and activities are working, and the criteria for determining success. Diagnosis tells us if we need to strengthen a weak ministry, eliminate it, or start a new one. The condition of our ministry will help us to determine priorities.

Integrate Purpose and Priorities

In seeking to establish priorities, a progression of thought and action begins with purpose and ends with establishing priorities.

The first step is to state the general purpose. Every church needs a clear purpose statement. This is fundamental. We need to know why we are here. This is true whether we are trying to arrive at priorities within the individual ministries or for the whole church. Each ministry (e.g., Sunday school, youth, women's organization) needs a clear statement of its purpose.

The second step in the progression is to isolate areas of concern. This is part of the diagnostic process. The best way to do this is to ask a select, representative group within the church or ministry, beginning with leadership, to list twenty-five needs of the church as those people see them. After the needs are listed individually, meet in small groups to take the individual lists, compare them, and produce a composite statement of need. If we are going to set priorities, we must know which areas need work and are of major concern.

The third step is to develop goals for each major area of concern. State the qualities we want to see. For example, if a major concern is our youth ministry, what qualities do we want to see developed? These might include discipleship, social opportunities, relevant teaching, or vision for outreach.

The fourth step is to develop specific objectives. This is difficult but essential. Developing objectives tells us what needs to be done to see the goals achieved. The objectives need to be specific, including a timetable and the people responsible.

The fifth step is to rate the objectives. Decide the relative importance of each, and ask what needs to be done now. As we consider the available resources—people, money, and facilities—a decision will need to be made. Every need will not be a priority. We must ask if we should proceed now and trust the Lord to provide the resources necessary, or wait. We will need to pray and then choose. The process means that certain needs will go unmet temporarily. But we will be pursuing the most important activities now.

Recognize the Value of Setting Priorities

The value of priority setting is inestimable. It affects the quantitative growth of the church because a church which is moving toward objectives is attractive to those outside. It projects an image of momentum. If an outsider senses that we are not moving toward effective ministries, he will not be interested.

Qualitatively, determining priorities will affect a church's leadership. Most people, even traditionalists, want things to operate effectively.

When they are challenged to think about choices and to set priorities, they will—if they are properly educated and motivated. Setting priorities strengthens confidence in leadership because church members know that people are praying about choices.

Because setting priorities forces a church to develop basic structures for ministry, as well as to train leaders, organic growth also occurs.

Action Items

List the top five priorities in your church. Do your leaders and members see these as priorities? If not, why not?

What barriers exist in your church to establishing proper priorities?

How can you overcome these barriers?

Bibliography

Engstrom, Ted W. *The Making of a Christian Leader.* Grand Rapids: Zondervan, 1976.

Kelly, Dean M. *Why Conservative Churches Are Growing.* Revised edition. New York: Harper and Row, 1977.

Ortlund, Raymond C. *Lord, Make My Life a Miracle.* Glendale, CA: Regal, 1974.

Richards, Lawrence O. *A Theology of Christian Education.* Grand Rapids: Zondervan, 1975.

6

Planning

A healthy church will never achieve its full potential with respect to growth unless its leaders fully appreciate, understand, and implement the management process. Management is an integral part of growth. Management includes, but encompasses far more than, administration. The difference between these two terms (as we use them) will become clear as we proceed.

Management is crucial to church health because of the nature of the church. As we have mentioned before, the church includes diverse needs; this gives it its complexity. Its members vary in age and spiritual maturity. The church includes married people, single people, the divorced, the widowed, and single parents. A healthy, properly functioning body will succeed in blending this diversity into a God-glorifying unity. Unity is one of the church's goals. For example, Paul prays in Colossians 2:2 that those who have not seen his face will be "united in love." Peter speaks of believers "... like living stones ... being built up into a spiritual house ..." (I Peter 2:5).

The biblical concept of management deals with the manner in which individuals fit, blend, or knit together without losing their uniqueness or individuality. This biblical concept of management includes everything needed to produce and develop a body of people. Management will involve leadership skills—motivating, delegating, training, planning, executing plans, organizing, administering, and doing anything else required to help a body of individuals realize its objectives and fulfill its purpose.

This explanation of management leads us to a rather sobering conclusion. The leadership role, which involves management, is carried out by the pastor. Unfortunately many, if not most, pastors are unequipped for this role. We are convinced that this is why so many churches never grow beyond a certain quantitative and qualitative level. The pastoral-training process aims at equipping a man primarily for the teaching part of the pastor/teacher office and secondarily for the pastoral role (if we limit the definition of "pastoring" to counseling, basic shepherding, and general pastoral duties). Usually our pastors are not equipped to perform managerial tasks which are essential if growth is to occur.

Part of the difficulty is a misunderstanding of definitions. Many pastors say, "My gift is teaching, not administration." That is perhaps a valid statement. Probably the pastor is equating administration with management and defining administration as paperwork and phone work. Since few people like paperwork, the assumption is that management skill is optional and that we can concentrate on teaching and preaching, which, after all, are synonymous with pastoral work. But we must see administration as only a small part of the management process. It can and should be delegated to people who do have gifts for administration. A pastor cannot delegate management because management involves the process of developing a united body of believers. If the pastor is not initiating, guiding, and controlling that process, the church will not grow. We must dispel the notion that management is somehow unspiritual. Management is necessary for the development of a healthy church. We do not underestimate the role of teaching. Ephesians 4:13–16 will not let us put a trifling value on the ministry of the Word. Preaching and teaching are central in church life. However, churches will not grow until pastors learn how to manage. Pastors need to balance the management and teaching functions.

We labor this point and this definition because this chapter will present planning as a nonnegotiable principle of church growth. Planning is vital in the management process. If we equate management with administration, this chapter will lose much of its impact.

As we begin to consider planning we must not see it in isolation. All of the principles involved in developing a healthy church relate to each other. These principles operate interdependently. For example, planning will be a futile exercise unless it follows purpose, diagnosis, and priority determination. By the same token, programming follows planning—in fact, is its twin principle. Programming and planning tell us how to reach the point where purpose, diagnosis, and priority determination have told us we, as a church, must ultimately be.

Practical Principles of Planning

We want to examine some practical principles involved in planning, keeping in mind that planning is a part of the management process. We must first define planning as it applies to churches. Planning is the definition and clarification of objectives, and the development of a specific strategy—programs, emphases, and events—which will help us to fulfill our goal.

An analogy will clarify our definitions of the words *goal, objectives,* and *strategy.* Any military planner will tell you that victory is predicated on three factors. Success involves a goal, objectives, and strategy. The goal is synonymous with purpose. In this analogy, the goal is to win the war. Objectives are the specific components of the goal. Objectives correspond to the hill to be taken, the city to be captured, or the river to be controlled. Strategy refers to the tactical maneuvers necessary to reach our objectives and thus to achieve our goal.

With respect to church growth, our goal is developing personal and corporate Christ-likeness. The objectives are specific characteristics— the development of unity, maturity, or fellowship. Strategy involves the specific steps (programs, emphases, and events) we take to reach our objectives. Planning relates to the third step, strategy. Planning tells us how to achieve the results we want, and sets guidelines for how long it will take to get results. Excellence is the fruit of planning. Without planning, the church is a maze of unrelated activities.

Planning Is Inseparable from Purpose

The first principle to remember is that planning is inseparable from purpose. We need to have clear-cut objectives—and a sense of purpose—for everything we do. Objectives also must be measurable. Achieving excellence is impossible when people are unsure about why they do things or what they are trying to accomplish. To plan without purpose is futile.

Since planning is related to purpose and objectives, a pastor who initiates the management process will spend a good deal of his time thinking about the future. Ted Engstrom, in *Making of a Christian Leader,* says, "Since no man can be sure of the future, why plan? Basically to improve the probability that what we believe should happen will happen. The point of the planning arrow figuratively touches the goal. The steps that need to be accomplished stretch back along the arrow into the present to create a plan."[1]

This principle of planning has been driven home in our church with respect to our building program. We had bought thirty acres of land and proceeded to design and construct the first phase, without a master plan for using the thirty acres. We did not think about estimating future attendance, or giving, or deciding the location and capacity of future buildings. The result has been an inadequate first phase. When we finally made a master plan, we discovered that the first building is in the wrong place and that its design is not functional. We are now paying the price for poor planning. Similar circumstances exist in other churches. A church must define its purpose and objectives, and plan accordingly.

Church leaders can relate planning to purpose by asking the right questions. Such questions make people recognize the need for planning and for clarifying objectives. Leaders need to ask themselves these questions:

What does the past tell us — for instance, what was our growth rate for the past ten years and the past five years?

Can we reasonably expect the church to grow at the same rate, or a greater rate, for the next five years?

If the church grows 25 percent during the next five years, what will that mean in terms of programs, facilities, and staff?

What do we want the church to be like, in terms of size and programs, in five, ten, or twenty years? What kind of staff and facilities will be needed?

What can we trust God to do, in addition to our projections about growth? What do we expect God to do?

1. Ted W. Engstrom, *The Making of a Christian Leader* (Grand Rapids: Zondervan, 1976), p. 141.

All of these questions and their answers will determine what plans you make to meet the needs created by what God does. If God is blessing your ministry, you will be constantly scrambling to keep up with Him. If you are not planning, you probably are not anticipating.

However, many pastors and church leaders have never thought this way and consequently find themselves mired in crisis management. An effective manager will make projections for the future and then work back to the present. A pastor must be a dreamer to the extent that he can think about the future and relate present planning to future numerical growth.

It is important to prayerfully consider plans for the future. We have suggested before that your church write, record, and publish a purpose statement. We also suggest that a church have written statements about specific, measurable objectives pertaining to attendance, giving, staff, and facilities. These are excellent topics to consider and pray about during a church-board retreat or at meetings of a master-planning or long-range-planning committee.

Planning Occurs on Two Levels

The second principle is that planning takes place on two different levels in a church.

The first level is planning that relates to the entire church. This kind of planning includes church government, staffing, facilities, and worship. It involves things which affect each member and each ministry. This planning should receive the bulk of the pastor's creative planning time because such planning involves large issues that affect the church.

The second level of planning is that done by the individual ministries. The people in charge of specific ministries (e.g., Sunday school) should be the primary planning initiators on that level.

The pastor's role will change as he relates to planning on these two levels. On the first level he will be the prime initiator, the creator, the dreamer, and the proposer. On the second level he will be the recruiter, trainer, motivator, helper, and resource person for those in charge of specific ministries. He equips leaders. As a church grows and full-time professional staff are added, those people equip others for the individual ministries. The senior pastor continues to plan on the first level, but encourages, motivates, and challenges from the pulpit to link everything together. His primary planning responsibility is the total ministry and the ministry of the staff.

Many pastors find themselves so busy planning and coordinating on the second level that they have no time to do creative planning. This is a danger signal. If the larger issues are not being dealt with, solved, and planned for, the church probably will not grow. A pastor needs to work toward freeing himself to plan creatively. He is not uninterested in or isolated from the ministry coordinators. But if the church is to move toward fulfilling its objectives and purpose, he must give attention to matters that pertain to the whole church. If he does not, no one will. The result is stagnation.

Planning Requires Time

The third principle of planning is that it takes time. Most of us plan intuitively on a regular basis. But we can relieve pressure if we schedule times to plan and to evaluate. To do this, we need a chart both to gauge what we must do to prepare for an event or activity, and to make sure all of the steps are placed on the calendar in advance. For example, if I am planning a men's evangelistic breakfast, I need to answer four questions.

1. How does this breakfast fit into the general purpose of the church?
2. What are the measurable objectives for the breakfast?
3. What needs to be done? This includes reserving a place, securing a speaker, establishing a budget, ordering materials, designing publicity, and organizing the program.
4. When do these things need to be done? Each item must have a date beside it. This insures that the preliminary work will be done, and done on time.

The importance of planning becomes obvious when you have several events, projects, and activities in progress at the same time. Often we say, "That event would have been so much better if I had had more time to work on it." Generally the problem was failure to plan adequately in advance. Proper planning is part of the process of translating your dreams into reality.

Planning Is a Process

A fourth principle of planning is that it is a process. We can look into the future but cannot accurately predict the future. Planning must be flexible and include evaluation. Sometimes, due to unforeseen circumstances, plans must be changed or abandoned. For example, we recently planned a major fund-raising campaign. As the event came closer, we evaluated our progress and decided that since our regular giving was lower than projected, we would be unwise to strain the budget by raising money for another purpose. We decided to postpone the event until later in the year. Evaluation needs to be done at strategic intervals in the planning process, as well as after the event. Remember the objective is always quality and excellence. Mid-course corrections are usually necessary and might include the allocation of more money, change in personnel, more publicity, or a change of date. Generally if the purpose, need, and priority are established, the planning will go smoothly.

These are the major principles related to planning. We suggest that a pastor or church leader read as much as possible about management in general and planning in particular. Books by Ted Engstrom and Lyle Schaller are among the best about these subjects. A number of outstanding seminars about management provide further training.

Guidelines for Assessing Resources

A planner, specifically a pastor or church leader, must ask three questions. All three relate to available resources after purpose, need, and priority are determined.

Personnel

What personnel are needed? Have you identified the people who will implement the proposed plan? Sometimes a plan will need to wait until God shows you who would be best to implement it. A pastor cannot take personal responsibility to do all of the work. He must involve others. This will involve delegation of responsibility. What if no one comes to mind and it seems as if no one is available to do the job? That may be a sign that the particular project is not a priority now.

Training

What do the personnel need to do the job? If you have recruited people to carry out the plan, what will they need from you in the way of initial training and continued motivation? Are the objectives clear to them? Are their job descriptions up-to-date? Do they know what you expect? Are there time limits? Sometimes we design wonderful plans and recruit able people, but discover that the person needs training and motivation that we do not have time to provide. The planner needs to count the cost in terms of his own time.

Budget

How much will the program cost? What is the budget? This is a crucial question. Every part of a plan needs a cost estimate. A good planner knows how to estimate costs and has up-to-date budget figures to tell him how much he can spend.

If these resources are not available, a planner needs to pray that God will provide those resources, or maybe delay implementing the program until the resources are available.

The Power of Planning

Effective and wise planning affects church growth in the quantitative, qualitative, and organic senses.

Quantitatively, a chruch which is meeting needs and moving toward objectives will be attractive and have a magnetic quality. Outreach events and programs will have a regular place on the church calendar.

Qualitatively, the church program will strive for excellence. Good planning and evaluation will insure effectiveness. There will be a sense of momentum.

Organically, leadership will be positively affected by effective planning. Responsibilities will be delegated to avoid an overworked group of leaders. A well-planned ministry will develop organizational structures which will change and become more complex as growth continues. Good planning will also further effective coordination or activity, which will affect the unity of the body. It will help communication as well.

Action Items

Plan one ministry (e.g., Sunday school or a Bible study) for your church. Complete the following planning analysis sheets, which provide a way to

recognize typical problems in planning and the symptoms of those problems. Included is a planning chart which will help you to organize a specific
activity.

Planning Analysis

Weak	Strong	Present Condition	Symptoms
		No real goals.	Church's purpose statement is not established/recorded.
			Members discuss goals, but do not act.
			Church does not acknowledge goals.
		No measurable objectives.	Objectives are not related to goals.
			Objectives are not measurable or specific, and have no time limits.
		Failure to anticipate obstacles.	Plans are not realistic.
			Completion dates are not met.
			People forget program plan.
			Crises are common.
		Lack of check points.	Completion dates are not set or met.
			Leaders do not know how program is progressing.
			Goals are short-term, and never have long-term effects.
			No plans have been revised recently.
		Lack of commitment.	People delay doing tasks.
			No priorities are determined.
			Planners miss meetings.
			No one submits reports.
			No one exhibits team spirit.
		Failure to effectively revise objectives.	Plans never change.
			No progress is made toward achieving objectives.
			Help is not sought when needed.

Weak	Strong	Present Condition	Symptoms
			Standards of the individual do not meet the objectives of the group.
			People waste time on programs that do not work.
		Failure to learn from experience.	People lose sight of goals.
			Feedback is ignored.
			Evaluation standards are not used.
			Church faces the same crisis again and again.
			People are unwilling to change ways of doing things.

Planning Analysis chart is adapted from material by Ed Dayton and Ted Engstrom; available from World Vision, Monrovia, CA.

Planning Chart

Goal for:_____

Purpose   For this reason: _____

_____

_____

Goal   We plan to accomplish this: _____

_____

_____

By this date: _____

We know it will happen because: _____

_____

_____

_____

Steps   We plan to take
          these steps: _____

                                _____

                                _____

                                _____

                                _____

People   These people are   _____
          responsible: _____

Cost   It will cost this   _____
          amount: _____

Bibliography

Engstrom, Ted W. *The Making of a Christian Leader.* Grand Rapids: Zondervan, 1976.

Getz, Gene A. *Sharpening the Focus of the Church.* Chicago: Moody, 1976.

Leadership Dynamics Seminar. Atlanta: Leadership Dynamics, Inc., 1977.

Mackenzie, R. Alec. *The Time Trap.* Paperback edition. New York: McGraw-Hill, 1975.

The Ministry of Management, Seminar, Training. Arrowhead Springs, San Bernadino, CA: Campus Crusade for Christ, 1972.

Schaller, Lyle E. *Parish Planning.* Nashville: Abingdon, 1971.

_____, and Tidwell, Charles A. *Creative Church Administration.* Nashville: Abingdon, 1975.

7

Programming

The principle of planning has a twin: programming. Programming is not identical to planning, but we call it a twin because the two principles are so inextricably related. Programming looks at purpose and objectives and plots the specific steps necessary to meet the objectives and fulfill the purpose. The specific steps include programs. Figure 2 illustrates the process.

Programming relates to diagnosis as well as to planning. In fact, our definition of programming includes diagnosis. We define programming as the part of the management process which takes the need isolated by diagnosis and meets that need through a specific activity.

Figure 2

The Planning Process

steps toward objectives

Facilities   Programs   Leadership

where we are

where we want to be
(objectives)

Purpose of Programming

The purpose of programming is to find needs and meet them. As we have seen with the other principles, confusion occurs in the church because members misunderstand definitions and purpose. Many times we have heard, even from pastors, "We are not interested in programs, only in people." That statement reveals a misunderstanding of the nature of programming and of people. Programs are vehicles to meet people's needs. The church exists for people. We are not interested in fossilized institutions within the church. But programs do not have to become institutions. Granted, they have a tendency to do so, but only when people lost sight of the purpose for a program. Every program in every church was instituted to meet people's needs. The purpose and the need may now be buried under layers of tradition and bureaucracy, but the program began with people in mind.

It is fascinating to read church history and to see the origin of many of our church traditions. Programs and activities were instituted because people in particular cultural settings had needs, and traditions represent honest attempts to meet those needs. Many needs were not evaluated properly, and the programs have outlived the need and remain as out-of-date institutions. This does not invalidate the need for flexible programming. Programming is not unspiritual or unscriptural. Its focus is on people and their needs. This represents the pattern of New Testament ministry.

The Scripture does not give us much help with programming. We are not told about many forms of ministry. This is why it is hard to do what many people talk fondly of doing: "patterning our church after the first-century church." The New Testament does not give a clear pattern with respect to specific program suggestions. The principles are clear, but God has given us latitude to develop specific ministries based on culture and circumstances.

In Acts 2:42 we are given a hint about several program components in the primitive church.

> They devoted themselves to the apostles' *teaching* and to the *fellowship*, to the *breaking of bread* and to *prayer*. (italics ours)

In this passage we read about four essential activities. We do not know specifically where or when they were carried out, with what frequency, or how organized they were. We do know that they were carried out to meet the needs of a great number of new believers in Christ who were beginning their journey toward Christ-likeness and needed a warm, loving fellowship in the midst of a hostile and pagan environment. Obviously the sheer numbers demanded some organization and some structure, but the forms that the organization assumed were not absolute. This is why the forms are not spelled out for us. If they had been we would try to imitate the form, not the principle, and cause ourselves many problems.

The point is that there is nothing incompatible between programming and the desire to minister to people. Programming is the vehicle to carry out a ministry. It is not an end in itself. It is the means to the end that people be developed into Christ-likeness.

Basis of Programming

The basis for programming can be stated in the answers to two questions. The first question to ask in approaching the programming task is, "Who are we?" This question is designed to help us to think about our corporate personality. Every church has a unique personality. It ministers in a unique cultural milieu. Its programs will be intended to meet the needs of its people. Your church will be attractive to specific people, because it ministers in its own cultural setting and it has attracted its own kind of people. Taking several considerations into account will help you to begin to understand who you are:

1. What are three unique or attractive things about the way we conduct evangelism, small-group activities, or other programs?
2. What is the general income level?
3. What is the general educational level?
4. What is the occupational pattern—blue or white collar; executive?
5. What is the predominant ethnic background?
6. Is the church located in an urban or suburban setting?

Answering these questions will help as you program to meet needs. For example, we have discovered that, because we minister to a large number of executives who travel extensively, our programs need to be short-term and self-contained. Long-term, weekly programs have generally been unsuccessful for us because our members cannot make commitments to them. But there is excellent response to short-term, need-oriented programs. A seminar about "Spiritual Leadership in the Home," planned for three Saturday mornings, will draw significant numbers of men. A six-month series that meets one evening a week would draw very few.

Your corporate personality will have other similar effects on your programming. If most of your church members are people from the lower income levels, you will find it difficult to evangelize and fold into your church those who are in the higher income brackets. You should program accordingly.

The second question which will form the basis of programming is, "Who's out there?" Most churches have not done a good job in analyzing or diagnosing their communities. We are not talking here about complicated, detailed demographic studies. Generally, what kinds of people, in what concentrations, make up your immediate community? Is your church located in an area where there are significant numbers of elderly or single people, college students, divorced or widowed people, or single parents? These kinds of groupings represent evangelistic programming potential. Your church may not presently include significant numbers of any of these groups, but a ministry aimed at them will attract them because of the needs represented.

Our church began a ministry for single people two years ago when we did not have a significant number of single people attending the church. The word quickly spread that here was a church interested in single people. Today we have 150 single people and the ministry is growing in quantity and quality. We are also located in an area with large concentrations of elderly people and college students. As yet we do not have significant programs aimed at these groups, but they represent future growth potential.

As you consider programming with respect to your community, remember the principle of priorities. The groups mentioned may not represent programming priorities right now. The point is that you should be aware of who is out there. If a church is to grow, it must have one eye on internal programming priorities and the other eye focused on the needs of its community. You will grow only as you can successfully attract people from the community. Need-oriented programming will attract.

The answers to these questions will provide a solid basis for establishing programming priorities. You cannot do everything now. You must be selective, and knowledge about your corporate personality and your community makeup will help you to make the right choices.

Design of Programming

We turn now to program design. Since we cannot do everything at once, how should we program for growth? This is an especially meaningful question for a small church to ask and answer, because generally it will have limited resources. A large church, with greater staffing potential and leadership resources, can reach out to more groups.

It is our belief that a church needs to do basic, internal program design and concentrate its leadership resources on the basics before it tries to develop specialized programs. This is because a church needs to have a magnetic capability to attract people if it is to grow. When a new person or family visits the church, he, she, or they will either be attracted by what they see and sense, or be repelled by what they see and sense. The most crucial part of a visit to a new church takes place in the car on the way home. "Well, what did you think?" If the children say, "I hated it!" the chances are that the family will not attend a second time and will select another church to visit next week. We are on trial. If we do not pass inspection by new people, we will not grow. A second visit is based on not only the friendliness sensed, but also on the seeming capability of this church to meet the family's needs. Programming is crucial to this positive impression.

One of the authors once was pastor of a very small church. No matter how hard he tried to reach out to the communtiy by visitation and door-to-door work, the church would not grow. The problem was not lack of visitors. It was lack of programs. There was nothing to attract and hold a family. There was not sufficient leadership to develop a basic family program. People would visit once and then make their way to a larger church which could provide a significant ministry to mom, dad, the children, and the teens.

Before a church begins to think of programs for unwed mothers or day-care centers, it needs to make sure that its programs minister to the basic family unit. We would suggest that basic program design should include ministries to men, women, couples, children, and junior-high and senior-high youth. This is not to say that other groups of people are not important. But the basic building block for growth will be the family unit, and this is the place to begin.

If a church determines to develop quality ministries to the family unit, that creates a problem. Many kinds of programs will attract men, women, and other groups. How do we select activities which will be attractive, yet not totally sap our leadership resources? To answer this question we need to reflect again on needs, for meeting needs is the purpose of programming. Two basic needs must be met in each of these groups. There is a social need. Acts 2:42 specifically mentions fellowship as an activity of the early church. People will be open to biblical content if needs for fellowship are being met. Those needs tend to be perceived more than any others. There is also a need for spiritual growth. This may tend to be more of a real than a perceived need at the beginning of a person's involvement. This would involve the need for teaching, for example. Basic programming should include the provision for fellowship and teaching, since they represent the basic needs.

Basic programming in a church might then include the following component parts. The objective is excellence.

1. Sunday morning worship
2. Sunday school for all ages, including adults
   a. Teaching
   b. Social activities outside of the class (for all age groups)
   c. Nursery services and staff
3. Men's social activity
4. Men's small-group fellowship
5. Women's social activity
6. Women's small-group fellowship
7. Couples' fellowship and social activity
8. Couples' small-group fellowship
9. Leadership training and development for all of these

This basic programming leaves many needs unmet, but if the above activities were happening in a church, the foundation would be there for greater development. We do not want to exclude anyone from the life of the body, but choices need to be made and priorities determined if growth is to occur. Your church may have available leadership in other areas; if so, use it. You may decide on different basics. Whatever you do, decide after you've carefully thought about and prayed about your diagnosis and priorities.

Before we discuss evaluation, we have a few suggestions about programs which should rate high on any church priority list. A boys' and girls' club program (e.g., Awana, or Pioneer Girls) has been attractive to parents as well as children. We believe this is a vital program. Also, ministries for elderly and single people should be high on a priority list, along with the development of an excellent adult Sunday school.

As the church grows, staff will need to be added in these basic areas. Our core ministry staff is developing this way:

1. Children's ministry coordinator
2. Youth (junior high, high school, college) coordinator
3. Adult ministry coordinator
4. Singles' ministry coordinator

As we continue to develop the staff, the college ministry will become a core staff position.

Evaluation of Programs

We come now to an important area, but one which most churches consistently overlook. This is the principle of program evaluation. The excellence of a church's programming, and thus its attracting capability, will rise and fall on its ability to properly evaluate its programs.

A church must be willing to evaluate. Since programming is based on need, and needs change, it follows that programming will also need to change. A church must recognize the need for evaluation.

Evaluation is difficult. If it is not done properly, evaluation may appear to be criticism. Our leaders must seek to promote and maintain excellence. If we are doing God's work and the lives of people hang in the balance, then our work must be done in the best way. In a volunteer organization it is not easy to insist on excellence.

Evaluation must be based on agreed-on objectives. Evaluation based on subjective criteria is devastating. This is why job descriptions are important for every job in the church. Recruiting has to include a careful explanation of the necessary time commitment, the exact duties of the job, objectives, and standards of performance.

Evaluation must not be equated with failure. A pastor told us recently that his wife had initiated a children's-church program. Sufficient help did not materialize, so the program was evaluated and finally ended. The reaction of a number of people was, "We told you it wouldn't work." The program was aimed at a need and therefore was valid. Evaluation showed a lack of resources, so the program was postponed. We have started, then stopped, many programs in our church. That does not mean they were failures. The timing may have been wrong or insufficient leadership available.

Evaluation will determine successful and unsuccessful programs. The criteria for success will not be only quantitative growth, although this will be a factor. Criteria will include:

1. The objective of the program
2. The need it is designed to meet
3. Continued existence of the need
4. Amount of time the program has operated
5. The program's attracting power (i.e., is it attracting people? Why or why not?)
6. The quality and needed quantity of leadership

There are other criteria for evaluation. For example, the church budget can be an evaluative tool. If a church practices zero-base budgeting, and a budget request is accompanied by a report about last year's ministry and a statement of objectives for the coming year, it will encourage self-evaluation. We also need to decide how we will define each of the criteria. For example, how will we evaluate a program's attracting power, or the quality of leadership, or a program's continued need to exist?

In our church, ineffective programs generally exist because of insufficient leadership, poorly trained leadership, or insufficiently committed leadership. If we decide a program is ineffective, we must take steps to improve it, replace the leadership, or discontinue the program. Whatever option we choose, it should never be seen as a negative process, but as a positive step to ensure growth and excellence. A helpful way to develop this is to build evaluation into the job description. Whenever possible, people should be recruited for a limited time such as six months or a year. After that, the person continues after mutual prayer and evaluation. This builds in the expectation for evaluation, and when evaluation comes it is not seen as personal criticism.

Evaluation is difficult because accountability usually is not part of the job descriptions of church workers. Even the pastor is not accountable to anyone. There is no clear standard of what constitutes acceptable performance.

The result of a lack of evaluation in the church is an organization that functions like the federal government, only on a miniscule scale. Programs are never challenged and so they become the possession of special interests and finally institutions. Succeeding generations of leadership do not share the vision and sense of need of the original leadership. There is no continuity of purpose from leader to leader. The same thing can be said of church constitutions and bylaws. They need to be periodically evaluated and changed (if necessary) to reflect present needs and realities.

Impact of Programming

Because programming is aimed at needs, it affects quantitative growth. As needs are met, people will be attracted and numerical growth will occur as a result. Quality is built into a total church program because selective development is taking place and the resources are being wisely used. This provides for future quantitative growth.

Qualitative growth occurs when a church has effective programming, because a church is doing a few things well. Needs for fellowship and preaching are being met, so personal and family growth occurs. The church is corporately growing and progressing toward Christ-likeness.

Because programming deals with the internal structure of the church, organic growth is implicit.

Action Items

Answer the following questions to help you to clarify the philosophy of your church.

What three words best describe our church?

What kind of people attend our church?

What makes this church unique?

What are the most attractive things about this church?

What is it about our church that appeals to people in the community?

To whom does our church have the greatest appeal?

To whom would our church like to appeal?

What programs and activities have been successful in the church? How do you measure success?

What is unique or distinctive about how our church does what it does in worship, education, evangelism, fellowship, administration, youth work, community relations, social services, missions, doctrine, finances, and staff? Also evaluate any other programs unique to our church.

What are the greatest strengths of our church?

What are the greatest needs or weaknesses of this church?

What must we keep in mind as we try to develop a philosophy of ministry for our church?

In one or two paragraphs, describe the philosophy (style) of our church's ministry. What is our corporate "personality"?

Evaluate the programs within your church, using the following questions.

List which programs are successful, and define how you measure success.

Which programs are ineffective? How do you measure this lack of effectiveness?

This item will help you to begin thinking about the effectiveness of current and future programming as that programming relates to people who already attend your church and to people who do not attend your church at this time. Using the charts that are included, decide on programs to meet needs of people within and without the church.

We will first consider programming to meet the needs of people in the church. In the column labeled "Types of people," list four distinct groups of people who attend your church at this time. For example, list young married couples, single parents, retirees, or deaf people. In column II, list three needs which you feel this type of person may have. For example, a single parent may need social contacts, child care, and teaching/counseling about rearing children. In column III, identify two programs, either already in operation or future possibilities, which would effectively meet the corresponding need. For example, two programs which would effectively meet a single parent's need for child care would be a Christian day-care center and a "Mothers'/Fathers' Day Out" program. Use column IV to make comments about the corresponding needs and programs you have suggested. Should the idea be pursued? Is current programming weak in this area? Who might be contacted to investigate this idea?

Next we will consider programming to meet the needs of people in the community. In column I, "Types of people," list four identifiable groups of people represented in your community. (They may or may not already

Programming to Meet the Needs of People in the Church

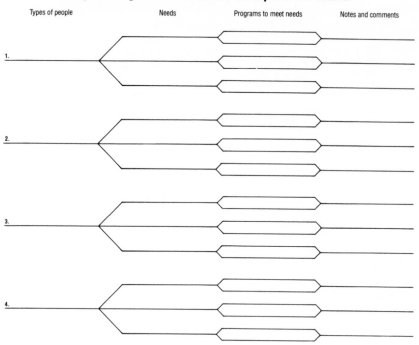

be present in your congregation.) Attempt to select groups you have not already mentioned in the previous exercise. For example, firemen, senior citizens, or lawyers may be significant groups in the community who are not currently affected by the ministry of your church. List three needs and/or interests that each of these groups may have. For example, senior citizens may need free-time activities, prepared meals, and financial aid. In column III, list two programs, either already existent or future possibilities, which would effectively meet the corresponding need. For example, two programs which would effectively meet a senior citizen's need for prepared meals would be a "meals on wheels" program and a weekly luncheon/social at the church. Use column IV to make comments relative to the corresponding needs and programs you have suggested. Should the idea be pursued? Is current programming weak in this area? Who might be contacted to investigate the idea?

Programming to Meet the Needs of People in the Community

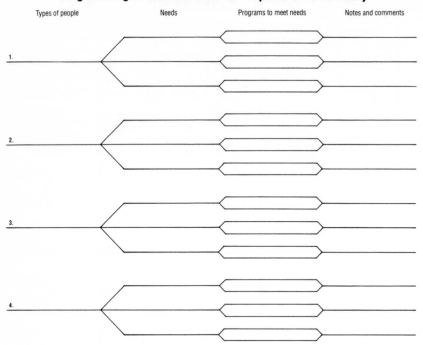

This analysis of needs and programming can be extended to include other significant groups beyond the eight you have listed. What action should you take as a result of the observations you have made concerning needs and programming?

This final item will help you to decide if it is possible for your church to begin some of these proposed programs. Use the rating scale that is included with the chart; indicate the ratings in the corner of each box, and explain the rating in the space provided.

Extend grid for additional options

-3 -2 -1 0 $+1$ $+2$ $+3$

Have Not | Have

Proposed Program Options

Resource Requirements

Leadership—Quantity/Quality

Leadership—Skills/Number

Space (Facilities)

Money (Budget)

Support Personnel

Conclusion

Further Assignment

Bibliography

Baumann, J. Daniel. *All Originality Makes a Dull Church.* Santa Ana, CA: Vision House, 1976.

Fickett, Harold L., Jr. *Hope for Your Church: Ten Principles of Church Growth.* Glendale, CA: Regal, 1972.

Pastors' Workshops. Charles E. Fuller Institute of Evangelism and Church Growth, Box 989, Pasadena, CA 91102. Action Items and charts for propsed programs are adapted from material in books 1– 4.

Perry, Lloyd. *Getting the Church on Target.* Chicago: Moody, 1977.

Snyder, Howard. *The Problem of Wineskins: Church Renewal in a Technological Age.* Downers Grove, IL: Inter-Varsity Press, 1975.

8

Climate

Every living organism depends on climate for its growth. Who has not had the experience of trying to care for a plant which would not grow or do well in spite of everything he did to make it grow? One of the authors recently bought a large plant for his office. He asked the saleswoman every question he could think of about the plant's requirements for water, food, and light. He took the plant to the office and followed the instructions faithfully and conscientiously. In spite of all that he did, the plant did not grow and in fact began to die.

Every morning as he entered the office he noticed one or more leaves had fallen to the floor. Finally, in desperation, he called the saleswoman and told her about his dilemma. She listened patiently and then asked a profound question: "Are you misting the plant?" He said no. She replied in a tone of voice which reflected her amazement that he would not have thought about such an obvious need, and proceeded to explain that this particular plant required humidity and that he should mist it every day. He thanked her, proceeded to find an empty Windex bottle, and misted the plant daily, admitting his skepticism all the while. To his amazement, after a few days, he noticed that the leaves had stopped falling off the plant and that several new leaves were appearing.

What had been missing? The plant was fed, watered, and received the proper amount of light. But a significant climate factor — humidity — had not been considered and was lacking. As soon as that factor was taken into consideration, the plant flourished. For other plants the amount of light or water would be critical factors in their growth. The experience with the plant illustrates the role of climate in the healthy development of every living thing.

The church, as we have pointed out, is primarily a living organism, not an organization. The church also grows healthily in a proper climate. Most church diagnosis does not include a study of climate (environment). Diagnosis tends to focus on quantitative growth and programming. Both are contributing factors, but certainly not the whole story. Every church should be evaluated in light of what it "feels like" to be a member of the church and what newcomers "sense" as they approach the church. Part of the reason diagnosis often neglects climate is that climate cannot be programmed, although programming affects climate. Climate is produced by prayer more than any other factor, because climate has to do with the spirit of the church rather than with a specific programming strategy.

Definition of Climate

We define climate in the church context as the combination of factors which determines how it feels to be a part of the church. Most of us, at one time or another, have visited churches in the attempt to locate a "church home," a church we can settle in and be a part of. Many people who have gone through this process have specific things they look for in a church (e.g., a good youth program or preaching). In spite of this list of specific expectations, the decision to come back to a church or the decision to join will be made on the basis of what someone sensed to be true about this particular church. How many times have we used this reasoning after visiting a church — "The preaching (or other specifics, such as Sunday school) was good, but the people didn't *seem* too friendly." Or, "I didn't (or did) *feel* accepted." Every church has its own corporate personality. If prospective members do not sense acceptance, warmth, and vibrancy, they probably will not be back. Many churches do not grow because a combination of climate factors produces a negative feeling; thus, people are repelled rather than attracted. Climate can be described by the term *attractive*. What is there about us, as a church, which draws people to us? Put another way, why do people come? These questions apply to Christians and non-Christians alike, although committed Christians will approach a church with a different set of expectations than will non-Christians.

This is important because it is the heart of the growth process. Why was Jesus' life so magnetic, and yet His church so often unattractive and even repulsive? The emphasis here is not on appearance. We are not merely trying to look good. The emphasis is on the spirit of His church, the genuineness and reality of its life. The church is attractive because it is genuine. People can sense the life pulsating beneath the surface of buildings, programs, and structure. They can also sense when the fire has gone out, when division and institution are paramount. This sense is devastating and repulsive.

Climate Factors

Three factors contribute to a favorable climate within a church. We will now explain those factors, and their components.

Love

The first and most important factor is love. Jesus, in John 13:35, makes observable love the new badge of discipleship when He says, "All men will know that you are my disciples if you love one another." The visible proof of the reality of their relationship to Him was to be the love among the disciples. He offers His own unconditional love for them as the model on which their love for one another was to be built. The command to "love one another even *as I have loved you*" (John 13:34, NASB, italics ours) makes the demonstration of love for one another an extraordinary expression. This expression of love was to be a certain kind of relationship, absolutely selfless and sacrificial in nature, which would be so unusual and so supernatural that it would constitute proof of the gospel message itself. How the church of Christ needs to be reminded of this power of love. The greatest attestation to the truthfulness of Jesus' claims was not to be in the academic discussion of their validity but in the observable demonstration of His life as shown in Christians' lives. In John 17:21, 23, Jesus prays that by the visible oneness of the disciples the world would know and believe that He came forth from God.

This kind of love has the potential to attract attention because it is so contrary to basic human nature. In Galatians 5:22, Paul begins his list of character qualities included in the "fruit" of the Spirit with "love." All of the qualities will be produced in the Christian's life by the Spirit. These qualities are supernaturally originated. This is essential to understanding how love works in the church. Love occurs naturally as all of us grow in our individual and corporate relationship to God. We are totally dependent on God's Spirit to produce love.

Part of the problem relating to climate in the local church is that maintaining love and unity is not as high on our priority list as it was on Jesus' priority list. We do not find these qualities on our prayer agendas nearly as often as finances, buildings, or programs. We feel that disunity, dissension, and strife are tolerable and can be overlooked. They can be only if we are willing to have our attracting power neutralized. Visitors sense nothing supernatural about most of our churches. The world's dominant impression about Christians and Christian churches is one of division and dissension. It is always interesting to see churches trying to design evangelism programs when the members cannot agree among themselves. The church today has a marvelous opportunity to express the love of Christ to the world through caring, giving, sacrificing relationships. The world is starving for genuine relationships. Loneliness and emptiness are major problems. The major attraction of many modern cults is perceived "love." Individuals sense a warmth and acceptance and are willing to believe whatever they have to believe as long as they can experience warm, genuine relationships. What a tragedy that many so-called evangelical churches repel people by a stifling, restrictive climate. These churches have nothing to offer. Jesus gave us a supernaturally produced love to draw people into the church. We ignore its importance to our own detriment.

Since love is defined for us in I Corinthians 13, the great love chapter, in terms that specify action, it will be helpful to examine several ways that love will be expressed in a local church. It is difficult to make a "love *is* _____" statement, but it is easy to make several "love *does* _____" statements. Love is described in I Corinthians 13 in several such ways. What kinds of actions within a local body of believers will contribute to an overall perception that will issue in statements such as, ". . . behold how they loved one another"? The answer to this question allows us to understand the climate necessary for the growth of a church.

Demonstrated among leaders

The first way that love must be demonstrated in a church is among church leaders (i.e., the pastoral staff and governing body). If healthy, caring relationships thrive among these people, the body will be affected. The observable love will filter down to other leadership groups, committee groups, and small groups until it permeates the entire body. Love must start with leadership.

Is there an observable love among the church staff? Is there a genuineness about this love or is the relationship strictly a professional one? If the relationship is a professional one, how does the church leadership differ from the leadership group of any other corporation or business? How can we expect the members of our governing bodies to honestly love and care for one another if the staff are like ships passing in the night? If you think we are exaggerating the problem, interview the pastoral staff of several churches. You will find frequent incidents of open competition, jealousy, feuding, and other evidence of division and dissension. Because several people work together in a spiritual ministry does not make them immune from the pressures to go their own ways and to do their own things. Church staff specialize in areas such as youth or Christian education. Their interests, gifts, and job descriptions do not naturally coincide. Wherever specialization is necessary, it will be easy not to be a body, not to be interested in the other ministries, not to pray for the other staff. Soon staff find themselves associating on a strictly professional basis. It is easy to feel slighted by the senior pastor or to compete for power. Love and unity on this level take a great deal of prayer and work because those characteristics are contrary to the normal relationships of those who specialize. A strictly professional relationship is inappropriate for a church staff, but often is the case.

The greatest challenge to a leader of a church staff is to develop relationships and communication in such a way that the rest of the body will thirst for such relationships themselves. If love does not start among the staff, the body will not reflect it. Model relationships among the staff do not just happen. The staff need to be together frequently on a social basis. They need to frequently pray together and study the Scripture together. One-day and longer retreats need to be planned in their schedules. Business and planning sessions will occupy much staff time, but if time is not given as well to social activities, prayer, and studying the Word, the church members will experience a dryness and vacuum in their relationships. The pastor and his staff must show that they love one another. If they do not, leaders of other programs within the church will not exhibit love for each other, and the entire church will lose its power to attract new members.

A second question concerns our governing bodies. Is there an observable love between the staff and the church board and among the members of these groups? The decision-making process involves the pastoral staff and the board. Does the same love evident among staff members permeate the board and affect its working and decisions? Are the members of these groups loving and caring brothers whom God is melding together with a beautiful oneness of heart and vision, or are they simply "sitting on the board"? What is the difference between the average church board and the board of a corporation or bank? Does the church board show a godly tolerance of differing ideas and opinions or do its members intrigue against and manipulate each other?

As is true on the staff level, love and unity among members of a church board are difficult to attain. When this occurs, it is attractive. Church boards work with difficult problems. Members represent various business and church backgrounds. For observable unity to exist in this diversity demonstrates the supernatural work of God's Spirit. How often this is not the case. Many boards are dominated by one or two strong people. To present a differing opinion or opposing view is to be personally opposed. Factions easily develop; power blocs win or lose votes. Recently a deacon in an evangelical church delivered a vicious commentary about several of his fellow deacons. The diatribe could have applied to the board of any large corporation. The church represented by that deacon is not growing, needless to say.

Many times, it is not only the intraboard relationships which suffer, but also the relationship between pastor(s) and board. We know about churches where deep philosophical and procedural differences between pastor and board were visible and acknowledged by the members of the congregation. We are not suggesting that differences will not exist or that issues are not difficult and decisions hard to make. What we are suggesting is that unless those things are dealt with in a climate of love and unconditional acceptance, the church will not and cannot grow quantitatively and qualitatively. God will not permit it.

With our mobile, busy lifestyle, attaining unity among the members of a church board will demand hard work and will mean additional time commitment. It is difficult to establish meaningful relationships if the board meets once a month. There must be time for prayer sessions, studying the Word, and social contacts outside of the business meeting.

We have found it profitable to schedule, in advance, one-day retreats for staff and church board members. During these retreats we focus on the Word and on Scripture dealing with our relationship to one another. It is beautiful to open the Word to a passage such as Hebrews 10:24– 25 (NASB) and meditate together about what it means to "stimulate" and "encourage" one another. We also try to find creative ways to do those things. After discussion about the passage, it is exhilarating to then pray about the passage. How much more love would be shown in our board meetings if time were spent to seek the Lord together? Does the church board come together to see which faction will prevail tonight on certain issues, or do its members come together to lay aside their favorite ideas and instead seek to do God's will? This climate will depend on what we do outside the board meeting.

"One another" relationships

The second way that church members demonstrate love is through obedience to the whole range of "one another" commands given to us in the New Testament. The Epistles amplify and develop the theme by commanding a variety of actions that manifest love. We are told to care for one another (I Cor. 12:25), stimulate one another (Heb. 10:24), encourage one another (I Thess. 5:11), bear with one another (Col. 3:13) and forgive one another (Col. 3:13). These words describe behavioral characteristics which show the meaning of love. These actions give content to the meaning of discipleship. These actions are to take place in all kinds of ways throughout the body at all times. Love represents encouragement, caring, rebuking, exhorting, stimulating, and many other things done in specific ways. These actions make love observable. If the world is to know about our discipleship it must be able to see our love for one another. We show our love when we minister to each other.

As is true of many other things in the local church, the New Testament does not give us forms for carrying out these activities. We do believe that we are on safe ground to say that these ministries will be evident in the small groups of the church. Genuine caring will not take place in a Sunday morning service. It will take place in leadership groups, committees, choirs, Sunday-school classes, or Bible-study groups. It will take place in these settings because it is in small groups that people will know each other, pray for one another, discern the needs of one another, and be in a position to minister to one another in the appropriate way. A visitor probably would not sense a loving climate in a church which did not have an identifiable small-group structure.

Care for visitors

A third practical way that Christians will demonstrate love is in the welcome and care of visitors. The love that members show for each other will carry over into the way church members approach the visitor. When love is honestly being expressed internally, visitors will sense a genuine welcome and concern. People will reach out to visitors because the richness of the fellowship that members experience will result in a genuine desire to fold as many as possible into that fellowship. Visitors who feel unwanted and unwelcome are being told nonverbally that "there is nothing here that you would want to be a part of."

A beneficial exercise for a pastor and the church leaders is to think about the whole Sunday morning program from the standpoint of a visitor. Most churches have a formal welcoming procedure—the greeters at the door and the "welcome" during the service itself. In addition to these things, can the visitor tell you were expecting him? If so, how? Are instructions and help available about where to go, nursery locations and facilities, and times of activities? Maybe you have never thought of these things as expressions of love, but they are explicitly so because they demonstrate a genuine desire to extend ourselves, and to reach out to others to make it easy for them to fellowship and live with us. We genuinely care for our visitors. We want them to come. Why? Because we are excited about what we have found. We want others to share in it. How tragic that in a community of love, people would go away feeling unloved and uncomfortable.

Do our church members want visitors to feel at home and to come back? Many do not. To some, visitors are a threat. They will break up our fellowship. We will get too big. Our intimacy will be destroyed. This attitude is mostly unspoken, but probably is more widespread than we would like to admit. Extending ourselves to visitors will mean growth. To many, growth represents danger because it will alter the status quo.

People need to be encouraged and taught to reach out to others. This involves training. Nursery workers, ushers, Sunday-school teachers, and others need to learn sensitivity and helpfulness. Visiting a new church can be traumatic. The experience should be pleasant and the welcome needs to express itself in a genuine helpfulness. People do not feel welcome by the mechanical things we do to welcome them (e.g., greeters at the door, filling out cards, or pulpit welcome). Visitors sense welcome when people go out of their way to speak to them and to help them. Everyone should be a greeter. Everyone should be alert to speak to those they do not recognize.

Unconditional acceptance

A fourth way we demonstrate love is not an action so much as an attitude. This means we unconditionally accept a person regardless of his spiritual maturity at a particular time. Many churches demonstrate the opposite. If Jesus accepted us on the same basis that we accept others, none of us would have a relationship with Him. He receives us "in spite of," not "because of." He is not exclusionary. He takes us as we are. His objective is always to make us resemble Him, but there is no possibility of rejection as we come to Him.

Generally, we exclude or reject people because they do not measure up to our particular standards. We fail to realize that in the diversity of the body of Christ, many maturity levels are represented. Some people have been Christians a brief time. Others have been Christians for many years. Some still are carrying baggage from the old life that the Holy Spirit has not yet dealt with. The Holy Spirit matures a person. He has His own pace for everyone. All of us are individuals. Disciples are not mass-produced. The Holy Spirit's timetable for me is different from His timetable for you. In the church, we tend not to accept someone unless he or she is exactly like us. He must be convicted about the same things, share my interests, and meet my standards.

Paul, especially in the Galatian letter, warns us about the deadly sin of legalism. Legalism is setting artificial human standards and trying to sell them as God's standards, even if we have to twist Scripture completely out of context to do so. Legalism, whether spoken or unspoken, says, "Unless you perform according to my (or our) prescribed codes of attitude and behavior, you will not be accepted here." Love appreciates how much of a change people have made from their old lives to their commitment to Christ. The church is the place for imperfect, unloving, immature people to grow spiritually. It is not the gathering place for perfect people. We must accept people genuinely. We cannot be critical and judgmental. Love gives people room to grow and the freedom to fall. It extends a helping hand to raise them up again. We need to learn to warn about sin, but not in a negative, hurtful way. So much of our preaching is negative and restrictive. Our objective is not to make people feel guilty because they are not like us.

How many times have divorced and separated people told us that they have gone from church to church without sensing a loving, supportive acceptance? People in these situations do not need more guilt. They desperately need to be ministered to, to be taught, and helped. Does this mean that we condone divorce or sinful behavior? No, because Scripture does not. It does mean that we will accept a person uncon- ditionally. If God has forgiven, so can we. We want to develop people. When rebuke and exhortation become necessary, we want to do it in a positive and constructive way. The climate of a church—what people sense and feel—will largely depend on the degree to which people sense an accepting, supportive corporate spirit.

Vision/Faith

The second factor we want to call attention to is vision/faith. We put them together because they are inseparably related. Faith, in this context, is a sense of corporate dependence on the Head of the church, Jesus Christ. We depend on Him for the resources to fulfill the vision that He has given us and the purpose to which He has called us.

Three qualities can be readily sensed about any local body of be- lievers. All three relate to vision/faith.

Sense of significance

The first quality is a sense of significance. Most people are attracted to a cause. People are drawn to scores of causes today. Specific causes appeal to people because those causes highlight needs and because they project real or idealistic solutions to problems. Causes also give people a sense that their energy is being expended in a significant way. To march for the abolishment of nuclear energy gives a sense of doing something incredibly important. Lives hang in the balance. There is a sense that if enough people march and protest, maybe some great ca- tastrophe can be averted.

The Communist Party has learned how to tap into the longing to be a part of something significant. The party has challenged millions of people to involve themselves in something which, from their point of view, has the potential to change the whole world and to improve the lot of all of mankind.

Jesus Christ enlisted men in the biggest cause of all. When He stood before the disciples before ascending to the Father, He challenged them to "go into *all the world*" (italics ours). He called them to a large job, a cause that was so significant that it would demand everything in terms of commitment and that all attempts to accomplish it would fail if God did not provide the supernatural resource.

People are attracted to churches that seem to move toward accomplishing a large purpose. God has called us to make disciples, to make a whole different person, to make new men out of dead men. Can there be a greater cause in all the world? What is the vision that propels your church? How big is your cause? If the pastor and leaders are not excited about the purpose and the objectives of the church, no one else will be either, and the nonmember will never sense that this group of people is on the move. Where does your church want to be in five, ten, or twenty years? Most people do not have time to be involved in a church which has the same number of people today as it had seventy years ago. For some reason that church does not seem to be moving anywhere.

Are people in your church being challenged to, enlisted in, and trained for involvement in what they sense is significant ministry? Every person must sense that his or her job is crucial to fulfilling the vision. This is why so many church workers are apathetic. They do not sense that their jobs are important. They do not see how their jobs fit into the bigger purpose. Why is a nursery worker or an usher important? How do those people fit into the big picture? People will wear out and dry out if not continually motivated about the vision. The vision gives significance to the job. That nursery worker needs to see that she is one of the first links in the chain that draws a new couple into the life of the church. The impression left by a friendly and competent nursery worker is significant in the decision to visit the church again.

Youth especially are challenged by vision. Many churches' high-school youth groups flounder because they do not offer anything significant. Our high-school students are motivated because they see the dozen or so public high schools around them as their mission field. The cause is bigger than they are. They pray and trust God for big things because the need is big and they sense a call of God to meet it.

Sense of expectancy

Faith is directly related to vision. Faith is a confession of dependence on God. We trust Him to do things. Faith is not an issue in many churches because faith implies that we are asking Him for something that we cannot provide for ourselves. Vision puts before us needs that are bigger than our natural ability to meet them. Faith asks for the resources to meet the need and depends on God to answer and provide. When our church purchased land, we bought thirty acres. We asked people to trust God for His supply. The prayer and the faith were based on the vision for a large, multiministry and multistaff church. The land was necessary to fulfill the vision. Without the vision, faith would have been unnecessary.

Faith provides consistent opportunity for people to trust God for things beyond themselves. Faith creates a hopeful, expectant spirit. We are excited about seeing God do things. We expect people to trust Christ, to grow in faith, and to become involved in ministry. A church with no articulated vision cannot demonstrate faith because there is nothing for which to trust God. Therefore the church lacks a sense of expectancy. Lack of expectancy leads to a "ho-hum" mentality. All of our energy flows into institutional maintenance—into keeping the parking lot in good repair and the lawn mowed.

An expectant and hopeful spirit can be immediately sensed. This is why it is so necessary to the climate for growth.

Positive spirit

A third quality that can be sensed is closely aligned with the second. When a group of people is caught up in what God is doing, a positive, constructive spirit results. People are attracted to positive attitudes. Throughout the Epistles the emphasis is on rejoicing, thankfulness, and similar attitudes. Even in testing and trial, a positive spirit is encouraged. How many of us have seen parts of churches where the spirit was negative, destructive, and separatist? The emphasis is on what we do not do rather than on the ministry of God's Spirit. In speaking with pastors, they often emphasize the problems, the difficulties, and the negative aspects of the ministry, rather than the positive ways in which God is moving. Much of our thinking tends to gravitate toward the negative.

One of the things we have found helpful is to regularly reflect on what God has done in the past and on those things, with respect to our vision, to which God has called us. We tend to bog down in the mire of current problems and to lose our sense of historical perspective. At one point our elders had been through a particularly trying period. They had been struggling with some intractable problems and were discouraged. At the beginning of one of our meetings, shortly thereafter, we began reflecting on what God had done in the past few months. After we enumerated various things we gave thanks to the Lord for those things. It was as if the cloud had lifted. We were rejoicing when before we had been grumbling. Our memories tend to be so short.

Do you emphasize, in your teaching and ministry, the things which unite believers or those things which divide them? Many people cannot be attracted to the church because all they see are denominational distinctions, and emphasis on money or separation from other Christians. A constant emphasis on denomination is repulsive, not attractive. Our "tag" affects our ability to reach out to and love a wide spectrum of people. People soon sense what is important to us. If the corporate sense is negative, exclusionary, and restrictive, visitors will know that.

Involvement

A third factor is involvement. People are most content and most positive when they are productively involved in ministry. A church whose members are involved in ministry will not experience the negative spirit and self-absorption of a church in which most of the people are spectators. A church with active members will experience less counseling demand because people will consider others and not their own special problems. Nonmembers will be impressed with the sense that people feel a strong commitment to the body and to its ministry. Bitterness and disunity will be at a minimum because the work load will be evenly distributed. One of the surest ways to improve a church's climate is to encourage people to exercise their gifts.

As you think about the three major climate factors — love, vision/faith, and involvement, you need to ask two questions:

1. How does it *feel* to be an outsider coming into our church?
2. How does it *feel* to be a member of our church?

If the answers to these questions are negative, you may have discovered the reason why your church is not growing. The quantitative, qualitative, and organic growth of the church will be severely restricted by negative climate factors. Your church may be like the plant referred to at the beginning of this chapter — dying because the climate stifles it.

Action Items

When members of your congregation pray together, do they ask God to do things because of His greatness and the sureness of His promises?

Do people tend to talk among themselves about all that God can do, or do they talk about the little that He might do?

Do members of your church behave toward each other as they are directed in I Corinthians 13:4–7? In what way?

Do members of your church believe that the congregation would support and stand by them during personal hard times, including times of spiritual struggle? To what extent? How would the church members show their concern?

Does your church see its faith result in God doing miraculous works (Heb. 11)?

Are people in your church *eager* to meet with each other for fellowship?

Do people in your church "stimulate" each other (Heb. 10:24–25, NASB) to show love and do good works?

Do the people in your church have a sense of holiness and urgency based on the knowledge of Christ's second coming (I John 3:3)?

Bibliography

Getz, Gene A. *The Measure of a Church.* Glendale, CA: Regal, 1975.

MacArthur, John, Jr. *The Church: The Body of Christ.* Grand Rapids: Zondervan, 1973.

Richards, Lawrence O. *A Theology of Christian Education.* Grand Rapids: Zondervan, 1975.

9

Leadership

Can you imagine people hungering and thirsting to know Jesus Christ in a personal way because they are so attracted to the people who are corporately called Christ's body? That can and should be happening in communities around the world. Scripture says that we Christians are called to be "lights" and "salt." Light illuminates and shows a direction; salt preserves and creates a thirst. People ought to hunger and thirst when they are around those who make up the body of Christ, the church.

However, these things will not happen unless those of us in the church do our part. We must be in the process of becoming Christ-like, and a congregation of such people will exhibit a vibrant expectancy, a life of faith, and a warm atmosphere.

Where are such churches? Is yours such a church? And what opens the door to such a dynamic community's development? We say it is leadership. "No," you say. "We have loads of leadership and yet our church is not exactly like that." But do you have loads of leadership, or loads of leaders? You can have many leaders but few who provide leadership. A leader is one recognized as such because of his personality or his position, but leadership is the quality that motivates and guides people toward objectives.

A church needs leadership. A ministry will rise or fall on its leadership. To the extent that a church can reproduce spiritual, effective leadership, it can enjoy biblical growth. The inability to develop such leadership is a major source of stagnation. Without this leadership there is no one to equip the rest of the laity to be involved in the ministry, and there is no corporate small group which models a lifestyle that creates a thirst within the church people—a desire to become bright lights and salt.

Broadening the Base of Leadership

This indispensable leadership cannot be developed unless a pastor demonstrates the likeness of Christ in his own life and thereby inspires and equips some people for leadership. In other words, the pastor must equip a few leaders who equip others. This continues until there is a base broad enough to build a bright and attracting ministry on. Then and only then will people hunger and thirst to know the Lord of lords.

We contend that a ministry will rise or fall on its leadership. David Womack makes this same claim in *The Pyramid Principle*. The principle states that "before a church may add to its mass of members and adherents, it must expand its base of organization and ministry (leadership)."[1] This is like piling sand on a table. You can pile on only so much sand before the table is covered. When you have no more space the sand starts flowing onto the floor. If you want and need to hold more sand, you must enlarge the table. That is the point of the pyramid principle: Add to the base and then you can expand the operation. Increase qualified leadership (and organizational structure) and then your church may grow, both qualitatively and quantitatively.

Attributing this importance to leadership is not new. Since the beginning of time, great things have resulted when great men have faced issues. Consider the leadership of Abraham, Joseph, Moses, Joshua, David, Peter, Paul, and Jesus. Where would the ministry of God be today if it were not for these men? Not only was the individual leadership ability of each essential in causing great works to occur, but also each man's ability to train other leaders was crucial.

Consider Joshua, if you will. Joshua responded to God's call to lead his people into the Promised Land. In Joshua 13:7–8 we read about

1. David A. Womack, *The Pyramid Principle* (Minneapolis: Bethany Fellowship, 1977), p. 79. Womack also developed the information about growth plateaus.

the predicament Joshua faced. He was old, the people of Israel were tired, and they seemed to be running out of momentum to conquer the land. So God in His infinite mercy and greatness gave Joshua a solution. He instructed Joshua to divide the land into tribal inheritances so that the task of subjugation would be spread to many small groups. This resulted in the involvement of more leaders, who gained great personal satisfaction (and other benefits) from conquering different parts of the land. God accomplished His end by raising up other leaders, through Joshua, to attack the task. Without these leaders, the task never could have been accomplished.

The same principle is true of the apostle Paul. After his conversion on the Damascus road, and the period of training that followed, he began to be an apostle to the Jews and then the Gentiles. Paul realized that he must expand his ministry if he was to reach the world. So he trained such men as Timothy, Titus, and Silvanus, who helped him train local leaders (church elders). These elders were responsible for carrying on and developing the ministry to the "uttermost parts of the earth."

Reaching Growth Plateaus

This kind of leadership brings about practical results. Research indicates that churches tend to reach plateaus at certain levels of attendance. Those levels vary, but generally the levels would be 50, 90, 120, and 250– 300; a slight leveling at 400, 600, and 800; and then a major leveling at 1,200 and 1,400. We will look at the causes and meaning of these plateaus in a healthy church.

The first level is fifty people in attendance. A church which grows to fifty people and then stops will be characterized by some or all of the following elements: doors closed except on Sunday, poor physical condition of the building, poor financial condition, pastor involved in physical upkeep, difficulty in paying bills, part-time secular employment for the pastor, and involvement of a clan or primary group (a group of relatives, normally, who have a great deal of control of the ministry). Resumption of growth occurs if the church frees the pastor to spend his full time in developing the ministry. Without his leadership skills and abilities, the church will remain at this level.

The next level is a regular attendance of ninety people. This size church is characterized by such things as closed doors, except on Sunday; a phone at the parsonage; a need for the pastor's wife to work;

little or no Sunday-school organization; the pastor's viewing laymen as a threat, not an asset; involvement of a clan in running the ministry; and discouragement of new people from coming back. At this stage, the pastor needs to come to see laymen as his greatest asset and gift from God. The pastor must use all his leadership skills to equip those laymen to become involved in doing the work of the ministry.

The third level is a membership of 120. At this stage, the church building is open all week; the pastor is furnished a parsonage and fair salary; the building is kept up reasonably; the pastor has surrounded himself with slightly trained lay workers; there are office hours with part-time secretarial help (probably the pastor's wife, without any extra pay); and the piano and organ are played well. In these circumstances the pastor should turn his attention to providing management and discipling skills for his most trusted lay leaders. Unless he can limit his responsible control to six or eight people who in turn work through other laymen, the ability of the church to expand and develop further will be greatly hampered.

The fourth leveling-off period is somewhere between 250 and 300 members. This plateau is characterized by a full-time secretary, efficient offices with a wide range of services, Sunday-school departmentalization, sermons with significant style and content, stability (the church is considered impressively large and yet comfortably small), a good salary for the pastor, and payment of all bills. At this point the church needs a different kind of organization. When a congregation is this size, it has taxed the limits of what one pastor can do. For a pastor to move his church from this point, he must not only cultivate better management skills himself, but also must have a second staff person, and then a third, and a fourth who are fully recognized team members. The first of these assistants should be one who can help with administrative tasks of the church through clearly defined lines of responsibility and authority. The church will continue to reach plateaus — 400, 600, 800, and/or 1,000 members — and each plateau will be caused by a new shortage of leadership. At each pause the church must increase its base before it can add to its mass. In each case this means the addition of staff members involved in actively equipping the lay people to do the work of the ministry, and in increasing the church's organizational complexity and sophistication. However, organization should be developed only as it is needed. Too much organization can kill a ministry.

The final level typically cited by church-growth specialists is the plateau of 1,400 members. Then the church faces a whole new set of problems which constitute a formidable barrier to growth. A church moves from a simple organization to a complex corporation. The need develops for sophisticated managerial leadership at the top, with effective business administration throughout the ministry. Unless a church has this kind of professional leadership, and unless these leaders can equip dozens and dozens of other leaders for the work of the ministry, the church will maintain this plateau indefinitely, or decrease in size.

This brief description of the pyramid principle and the various growth plateaus should be sufficient to establish the need for organic growth. Quantitative and qualitative growth depend on a continually expanding leadership base. A movement will grow only as leadership is developed. The "... equipping of the saints for the work of service ..." (Eph. 4:12, NASB) has to be at the top of the pastor's priority list. He cannot do the work alone. In spite of this biblical and practical imperative, he often finds qualified leadership a scarcity and finds himself unable to discover or develop it. How does the pastor begin this development process? If he does not equip leaders, the church will not grow and the pastor will find himself unfulfilled in the ministry.

Diagnosing the Present Leadership Situation

Solving the dilemma about leadership depends on diagnosing the present leadership situation in the church. You will recall that diagnosis is the analysis or evaluation of an area of ministry based on relevant factual data. Every church and pastor can profit from regular analysis of the church leadership situation.

Analysis of Needs for Leadership

To analyze present and future leadership needs, we must do several things. First, make a list of every ministry position now being filled in the church. The list would include Sunday-school positions, committee chairmen, youth ministry positions, and the governing body. Then make a list of every ministry position which now needs to be filled, given the present attendance level. These are in addition to positions presently filled. For example, in your Sunday-school leadership structure you may have all but the superintendent and fifth-grade teacher positions filled.

These two positions would go on this second list. Finally, make a churchwide organizational chart which reflects present positions. This chart will make the unfilled positions obvious. It will also show relationships and who is accountable to whom.

These three procedures will help you to see which positions are filled, which need to be filled, and how the positions relate to one another.

You also need another list that shows future leadership needs you will face when your church reaches the next plateau. For example, if your attendance increases by an additional 200 people, what additional leadership will you need to provide for new ministries and for the expansion of the old ones? A growing church has an insatiable thirst for leaders. You will always need more than you have. Try to project future leadership needs so that these needs can be prayed about, and qualified people sought and trained.

In compiling these lists, remember that you are analyzing leadership needs. Do not list every involved person. List only the committee chairman, or the Sunday-school department head.

Analysis of Leaders

We need to analyze present leaders and the kinds of people we need for the unfilled leadership positions. Several questions should be answered in evaluating leaders.

1. What kind of person is needed for each position? Do we need someone to take charge of a ministry, an assistant, or a support person?
2. What kind of skills does a person need to do a good job in this position? Are the skills interpersonal, technical, managerial, or a combination?
3. What are the person's strengths and weaknesses as those qualities relate to the job? Do the strengths outweigh the weaknesses? Are the weaknesses related to spiritual issues? (One of the Action Items for this chapter will help you to evaluate a person's strengths and weaknesses).

The point of this diagnostic process is that you do not want merely to fill jobs, but you want the most qualified person available.

Leadership Problems

Several leadership problems merit special attention. Probably every pastor has faced one or more of these barriers. We will list six problems and attempt to suggest creative ways to solve them.

Leaders Are Aged

"I have men on my board who have been in the church for years and who will not accept any new ideas."

This is a particular problem in many churches with a long history. Young pastors attempt to move churches in new directions but find their efforts thwarted by factions of their leadership who seem to be interested in institutional maintenance and carrying on tradition. Sometimes aged leaders seem to be obstructive, but simply have not been approached or worked with in the right way. Many times we tend to propose new programs and methods before adequately preparing our leaders. Here are some suggestions:

1. Deal with the individual personally.
2. Determine whether the individual opposes the idea on philosophical and biblical grounds or if the resistance is due to tradition.
3. Outline the problem or need which your idea will solve or meet and ask for his or her suggestions about possible solutions. Suggest your idea as a possible way to solve the problem. Make sure the person understands the problem before you offer solutions.
4. Seek to deal with the problem biblically and philosophically. If a person sees the biblical mandate, generally he will be amenable to different solutions.

The point is that we must not propose new ideas suddenly, and not, for the first time, in a group setting. Preparation is needed.

If preparation for change or creativity occurs in the right way, you may only need time to sell the ideas. When leaders have outlasted six pastors and survived three church divisions they tend to be skeptical of new ideas. It will take time to develop trust so your ideas can have a fair hearing. Prepare before you propose, pick your issues, and be prepared to take the necessary time to see your ideas implemented. If it becomes obvious that there is a genuine obstruction, you have two possible courses of action.

First, be prepared to wait, all the while working with and preparing younger people to move into leadership positions. Replace the old with the new. This takes time and a gentle, patient procedure that will not cause division and hurt feelings.

Second, if this is not possible and younger people are not available, you may have no other choice than to leave. In extreme cases, not only is the leadership aged, but the whole congregation is also aged. If this is the case, and there is not a younger manpower pool from which to draw and prepare future leaders, there may not be much potential. A church must include different age groups. For example, young couples attract other young couples. Sometimes a young pastor will attempt to work with a congregation that has predominantly older members. Such a church will have difficulty growing because growth potential is not there.

Michael Tucker's *The Church: Change or Decay* deals with effecting change in a stagnant, traditional church. We recommend this book.[2]

Leaders Are Unavailable

"I have key jobs to fill, but don't have the right people."

All churches have positions that need to be filled, but somehow we cannot find the perfect person for the job. This is especially true in a growing church with a constant demand for new leadership. But sometimes the problem is that we do not have a way to find the right people. If God has called us to carry on certain ministries, He will provide the right people. If this problem exists, three things may be true.

We may not know who is available. There is no way to gauge the interest and skills of our people. There is no specific recruiting process.

The people may be available but there is a "spectator mentality." This is a spiritual issue and a biblical one. It needs to be addressed on that level.

The job does not need to be filled now. There are jobs in our church that need to be done, but we are not doing them because there is no

2. (Wheaton, IL: Tyndale, 1978).

one qualified to do them. Maybe the time is not right. We need to rely on God to meet such needs.

Leaders Are Spiritually Incompatible

"I have men or women in leadership positions who are bitter and unforgiving toward one another."

This is clearly a spiritual issue. Nothing will sap the spiritual vitality of a church more than the toleration of this attitude. It must be dealt with and the gravity of it made known to those involved.

This problem is especially significant because, if it is not dealt with, God will not bless your ministry. The best way for a pastor to solve this problem is to deal directly with these people, using the principles of Matthew 18. It is the pastor's duty to initiate the process.

We know of a case in which a pastor did that. One man in his congregation was influential in two ministries, but, in subtle ways, refused to cooperate with the pastor. The pastor talked to us about this, noting that his church was not growing and that his own daughters had drifted away from the church. We told him that unless he confronted the man, nothing would change. He did as we recommended, and later told us that the man had admitted his faults. Since then, the pastor said, the church added thirty new members in two months, and his daughters returned to the church.

We encourage church members to work to change bitter or unforgiving attitudes. One aid to this is John Alexander's *Practical Criticism: Giving and Receiving It*.[3]

Leaders Are Untrained

"I have potential leaders, but do not have the time or ability to adequately train them."

The pastor cannot be expected to have all the skills necessary to meet all the needs for training people to serve. A pastor has three options for solving this dilemma.

Consider hiring additional staff. The church which has consistent

3. (Downers Grove, IL: Inter-Varsity, 1976).

unmet training needs probably has reached a growth plateau and needs additional staff. Staff specialists in various areas of ministry can take the responsibility for training lay leaders.

Utilize other training resources outside the church. There are seminars, institutes, and other training resources to which people can be sent. Also, try to determine where a particular ministry is being done well and send the untrained person to that location to observe and learn from people who are already doing it.

In addition to these suggestions, you may need to do the best you can to nurse the leaders along and let them learn by doing. Provide whatever time you can, assure them of your support and counsel, and let them learn by trial and error. There are many jobs in the church that none of us have any experience in doing. But we talk about needs, begin to trust the Lord, step out, and minister. All the while we are looking for resources which can provide the necessary training.

Leaders Are Uncommitted

"I have people in leadership roles who have no seeming commitment to the task or the church."

This problem is particularly devastating. It sometimes occurs in a church with an extreme congregational form of government. If many positions are filled with elected rather than appointed people, this problem will recur. If this is the case and cannot be changed, the best thing to do is to emphasize the church's vision and purpose and to try to stimulate, in small groups and in personal interaction, a sense of commitment and responsibility. Work with job descriptions and standards of performance so that the person knows what is expected of him or her. The problem may be a lack of understanding of the church's direction and purpose.

Leaders Are Unqualified

"I have leadership positions filled each year by people who are elected to do the job but do not qualify in their lifestyles and skills."

This is a frustrating barrier to growth. There are two solutions to it.

First, try to change the constitution so that more leadership positions can be filled by appointment rather than election. This probably would be a time-consuming process and would be much easier in a new church than in an established one.

Second, if it is not possible to change the constitution and form of government, do whatever you can to strengthen the nominating procedure to guarantee that qualified people are being nominated. Impress on the governing body the need for qualified people. Nothing will be more frustrating than having unqualified and uncommitted people in leadership positions and not being able to do anything about it except hope for better at the next election.

There are other leadership problems in addition to the six we have suggested. Many of these will not be solved overnight. All we have attempted to do here is to describe the importance of developing qualified leadership. Everything depends on it. It is the pastor's most important task. The ministry will not only *not* grow without it, but will also stagnate.

Developing Leadership

In the long-range process of developing leadership, several factors will be helpful if kept in mind. Leadership develops in the context of climate. There must be a climate for involvement. Some structure must exist for recruitment and involvement. Some way must be found to discern interests, gifts, and skills. A survey is helpful. Preaching and seminars about using spiritual gifts and emphasis on the importance of involvement in ministry are crucial.

In recruiting, look for five qualities.

The first of these is a person's willingness to learn. We do not need people in any leadership position who are not open to new ideas or suggestions and who will not take direction.

The second quality is faithfulness. I Timothy 3:10 tells us that before a deacon is appointed he is first to be "tested." The best way to determine faithfulness is to gradually move people from minimal responsibility to more significant responsibility. If a person is not dependable and faithful in the small jobs, it is doubtful that he will be in the larger responsibilities. Another way to test faithfulness is in the context of the small group. This is a good place to observe consistency, spirit, and other qualities.

Third, we want people in every position who have a heart for the Lord and who will conduct their ministry in a spiritual way. We want people who are growing spiritually, who are in the Word, who desire to minister to the needs of others, and who see their ministry as a service and not a duty to be performed.

Fourth, time is an important factor. So often we recruit people without explaining how much time a ministry requires. Try to give people a realistic idea of the time commitment that will be necessary to do the job. This will attract some people and eliminate others, but you must know if the person can spend the necessary time.

Fifth, every person who makes a commitment to the church, especially to membership, has certain interests, skills, and gifts which can be utilized in a ministry to the body. The person who joins the church becomes part of the manpower pool and is a candidate for some kind of involvement. Find what those interests are and involve the person as soon as possible.

Removing Volunteers from Leadership

Pastors not only must find people for leadership positions, but also must remove unqualified, uncommitted peoople from leadership positions. This problem involves the whole question of how one goes about creating a sense of accountability in a volunteer work force. In many churches, accountability simply does not exist. When many positions are elective ones, the problem is compounded. The pastor finds himself dependent on undependable leaders or leaders who do not have time to do what the job requires. Several things are important to keep in mind about this common dilemma.

Each person needs to know whom he or she *reports to*. An organizational chart will help. This simple matter stimulates accountability. If I know that someone is responsible for me and that there is someone to whom I can go for encouragement or problem solving, it will make a difference in accountability. A pastor recently told us that for the first time his church made an organizational chart. He is the pastor of a church with 700 members. Some leaders had no idea about their relationships with other people, or to whom they were accountable.

Every person, elected or appointed, must have his duties explained to him before he begins a job. If that person cannot fulfill the job requirements and/or qualifications he has a chance to remove his name from consideration. Every position needs a description. The expectations about time required and criteria for measuring results are spelled out ahead of time. This is especially important if the position is an elective one. Once the person is elected, he is in office until the next election.

After a person is elected or appointed to a leadership position, he meets regularly with the person to whom he is accountable. They enjoy fellowship, review progress, discuss needs, budget, and personnel, and plan for the future. Midcourse corrections are made, based on goals and objectives.

If a person is not demonstrating faithfulness, he should be confronted about the reason for lack of progress. It may be due to lack of time, misunderstanding about the job, lack of training, or any number of other reasons. The reasons should be pinpointed. The way those reasons are pinpointed is important to a continued relationship with the person. Explain that you know the person wants to do a good job, and that you want to help him to do a good job. If time is the reason for lack of performance, you might say, "If time is the problem—and it appears to be—I think to be fair to you we should find someone else to do this job and find an involvement for you which will not take this amount of time. I want to relieve you of the pressure."

In confronting people, it is important for them to know that you want to help them, that you want to help them find the best place to serve, and that you want to help them acquire more training and skills. If the problem is a spiritual one, it needs to be dealt with biblically.

The whole issue of volunteer accountability has not been faced in most churches. Pastors and leaders find it difficult to confront volunteers. Admittedly it is a difficult issue. We need to begin to foster the sense of accountability. The quality, excellence, and depth of ministry depend on it.

Leadership and Growth

Quantitatively, much depends on leadership development. If new people visit a church but find that lack of leadership hinders a ministry, quantitative growth will stop or slow down. Organic growth must develop to maintain quantitative growth.

Qualitatively, everything depends on leadership development. Ministries to adults, youth, and children must be adequately staffed with qualified people. The work load must be equitably divided to avoid overworking a few people. Depth of ministry depends on the extent to which people minister according to their gifts. Training must take place at every level. Teaching excellence must be maintained. Sunday school, Bible studies, seminars, and Sunday services must have qualified teachers and leaders, who are recruited from among church members or people who regularly attend the church.

Organic growth must keep pace with quantitative and qualitative growth. Churches must recruit people, involve them in ministries which test faithfulness, and then give them greater responsibility. Full-time staff will be added at strategic points to provide training.

Action Items

What plateau is your church experiencing? What causes the plateau and what are the solutions?

Go back to the point in the chapter that dealt with diagnosing your present leadership situation. Diagnose the leadership situation in your church.

This chapter includes a list of leadership problems in the local church. Is your church experiencing any of these leadership problems? If so, what can you do to solve these problems?

What specific steps can you take to improve your effectiveness as a leader?

In this chapter, we said that churches must analyze whether a person is suitable for a leadership position. Rate candidates for specific positions on a scale of one to five, with five being the maximum. These are the criteria: spiritual life; experience and background; vision for the job; appearance; whether he or she is a self-starter; skills (interpersonal, leadership, managerial); availability; need for training; and schedule (whether he or she can commit enough time to the position). A person may have a low score in one area and high scores in all the others. Does the low score disqualify the person? If not, he or she is probably a good candidate for the job.

Bibliography

Benson, Dan. *The Total Man*. Wheaton, IL: Tyndale, 1977.

Getz, Gene A. *The Measure of a Man: A Practical Guide to Christian Maturity*. Glendale, CA: Regal, 1974.

Halverson, Richard. *How I Changed My Thinking About the Church*. Grand Rapids: Zondervan, 1972.

Leadership Dynamics Seminar. Atlanta: Leadership Dynamics, 1977.

Womack, David A. *The Pyramid Principle*. Minneapolis: Bethany Fellowship, 1977.

10

Laity

The health of a church will exist in direct proportion to its laity's involvement in the ministry of the body. Noninvolvement of laity in the ministry is a serious disease of the church. It is a hideous disease which attacks the church's vital organs. As we have seen, noninvolvement is a major climate factor. Unless the biblical cure is discovered and applied, this disease will prove fatal. Involvement of every member in meaningful ministry is such a clear biblical principle of ministry that not to emphasize it and not to build our ministries on it is either to be ignorant of the clear teaching of Scripture or to be willfully disobedient to it!

But most churches ignore this principle. Pastors try to do all the work of the church, to their own and their families' detriment. Even when pastors become sufficiently impressed with the biblical imperatives, they run into a stone wall when they try to implement those imperatives. Church members think that the people *hire* the pastor to do the work. This attitude is so ingrained in many churches that the pastor feels that to ask for lay involvement in ministry is an imposition. The people correspondingly feel that their involvement is a favor to the pastor. This constitutes the worst kind of disease because it is a direct and clear violation of the biblical pattern of church ministry and organization.

126

Lay Involvement Indicated in Scripture

First we want to consider what Scripture says about lay involvement. Two major passages clearly spell it out. The first is I Corinthians 12– 14. Every believer has a personal responsibility to fulfill in the context of the body. This responsibility, as stated in these passages from I Corinthians (italics ours), has been given to him or her by God.

... to *each* man ... is given for the common good. (12:7)

... and he gives them to *each* man, just as he determines. (12:11)

But in fact God has arranged the parts of the body, *every* one of them, just as he wanted them to be. (12:18)

We see from these verses that each and every person is responsible for exercising his or her own personal talent(s), given as a gracious gift from the Spirit Himself. What a positive revolution would occur in the average church if laymen would begin to see that God, not the pastor, has entrusted them with special gifts to be used conscientiously in the body. What a radical redistribution of the workload would occur! It is not a matter of the pastor trying to get out of work. If we could only see that each of us has a specific and God-given role to play. Every layman is called by God to minister. We are fond of discussing the pastor's call to preach. The truth is that each of us is called to a specific, fulfilling, and vital ministry.

The purpose of the distribution of gifts by the Spirit is the common good.

... for the *common* good. (12:7)

As it is, there are many parts, but *one* body. (12:20)

so that there should be no *division* in the body. ... (12:25)

All of these must be done for the strengthening of the church. (14:26)

The principle in this whole section of Scripture is unity in the midst of the diversity present in the church. The objective is the building up and proper functioning of the whole body. This can occur only by the proper functioning of each part. Ephesians 4:16 makes it clear:

From him the whole body, joined and held together by every supporting ligament, grows and builds itself up in love, as *each* part does its work.

God has designed the church in an ingenious way. It is, as we have seen, an institution that makes disciples. As such, it includes people of varied background, maturity, presupposition, and expectation. How can unity be maintained in the face of such diversity? Simple. Equip each person with a spiritual gift to contribute. Let the contribution be made in a climate of love, care, and acceptance. The growth of the body is accomplished in a way that is amazingly attractive to those who are on the outside looking in.

The failure to contribute according to one's gift causes the breakdown of the church's internal structure.

> The eye cannot say to the hand, "I don't need you!" And the head cannot say to the feet, "I don't need you!" (I Cor. 12:21)

The passage goes on to explain the interdependence of the parts of the body. What happens when one leg is paralyzed? It forces the other leg to do the work of both legs. The muscles in the healthy leg become large, hard, and overworked. That leg has to compensate for the paralyzed leg. Consequently the whole body suffers.

By analogy, many parts of the body of Christ are paralyzed. This forces the contributing members to overcompensate and overwork. How many times we have seen a few people doing the bulk of ministry in a church. This condition has devastating implications with respect to climate. The overworked members become resentful and bitter about the situation; eventually they become critical and judgmental. Division and disunity attack the church. When this happens, the game is over. Institutional maintenance is all we can hope for. Apathy and passivity set in and no amount of increased effort by the pastor or handful of workers can change it. We will deal with more of the implications of this condition later.

Now we want to consider a second passage of Scripture (Ephesians 4:11–16) which reinforces and enlarges on some of the aspects of I Corinthians 12–14. Where Corinthians deals with the involvement of each member of the body, Ephesians 4 focuses on the pastor's duties. Verse 11 tells us that God has given gifted men to the church. Verse 12 (NASB) tells us what they are to do.

> . . . for the equipping of the saints for the work of service, to the building up of the body of Christ.

This passage beautifully complements I Corinthians 12. It reinforces the pattern given to us in I Corinthians 12.

The pastor/teacher has as his primary focus the "equipping" of the saints for the work of service. The pastor is to help to equip the laity to do what God has called them to do. This is a reversal of the usual operational pattern existing in the church today.

The passage goes on to expand the definition of equipping. In verses 13– 15 Paul concentrates on the role of the pastor in leading the flock into spiritual maturity. Probably this involves exposition about the meaning of Scripture. People not only are given jobs to do in the body. There is also a corresponding growth into maturity. The pastor is responsible to lead in this process. He does this, however, in the context of the growth of the entire body. The growth of the body depends on the proper involvement and function of each individual part (v. 16). The pastor not only unfolds the meaning of Scripture, but also oversees the whole management process by which the saints (v. 12) are involved in fulfilling ministry according to their God-given abilities and gifts.

Many pastors think their responsibilities begin and end in the pulpit. Not so! Leaders must help to adequately challenge and train believers for ministry. Obviously the pastor cannot do all of the challenging and training, but he must be the catalyst to see that this is done. Not every pastor is gifted in developing leadership and overseeing the process. If this is the case, God will need to provide others who can give impetus to the process. However the process is structured, believers must be encouraged to minister.

If a body, especially the leadership council, resists this principle, the pastor, leaders, and members need to thoroughly study Scripture and think about the implications. People have to see that this is not a personality quirk in the pastor, or an indication of his laziness. By biblical definition, he is a player-coach. He is there to help the saints to do *their* ministry more effectively. Any other pattern will eventually result in stagnation and death. How many exhausted pastors and discouraged, frustrated church leaders will we discard before we see and deal with this issue?

Implications of Lay Involvement

The implications of the biblical pattern of lay involvement are enormous. We want to consider several, some of which we have already mentioned.

If every member is involved in the ministry of the body, this will affect our definition of discipleship. The word *disciple* occurs repeatedly in the Gospels and the Book of Acts. It never occurs in the Epistles. Why do we not find this word in the Epistles? We believe it is because the Epistles present a new concept of discipleship. We often define "discipleship" in a technical way (i.e., the intense preparation of leaders). This is what Jesus did. This is also what Paul did with Timothy and others. Today parachurch organizations that work primarily with homogeneous (students or military people) communicate a technical discipleship.

The Epistles, while focusing on preparing leaders, give more attention to discipleship as that applies to each believer. Developing people into the likeness of Jesus Christ is a function of the whole body. This is why there is a whole range of "one another" ministries. We are built spiritually by being exposed to those who exercise the ministries of service, teaching, leadership, and all the other gifts of the saints in the body. We are what we are today because of the influences of many people. That is why it is difficult, if not impossible, to transfer a parachurch discipling *form* of ministry into the church. Within the body, there are diverse needs which can be met only as we are exposed to varying gifts. We thus find it necessary to spend concentrated time with leaders. Technical discipleship has a place in the church structure, but we do not see a biblical mandate for every believer to be involved in an intense one-on-one relationship with another in order for discipling to take place. God has provided beautifully for discipleship in the "one another" ministry of the body. Everything that happens in the body contributes to discipleship. This is why paralyzed parts of the body are such an issue. Those parts are not contributing the ministry of their God-given gifts to others. They are not contributing to the discipling of others. Others are not benefiting from the input of their lives. Consequently growth is not occurring properly. Grotesque mutations are the result. Each of us is built by the teaching of one, exhortation of another, the help of another, the rebuke of another, the faith of yet another. We are discipled by our brothers and sisters. No *one* discipled us. We are built by music, by books, by a host of other influences. To grow as balanced, mature, godly persons we need the influence of all the gifts in our lives.

If every member of the body is to be involved in fulfilling ministry, we must design an effective structure for gifts to be recognized and exercised. Is it easy to get involved in your church? Probably many people have never been involved because they have never been asked to do anything and may not realize they have something to contribute. This is a larger implication than we may realize. We need to examine our attitudes about using our gifts. We need to answer several questions.

Are we convinced, biblically, that every member has an obligation to contribute?

Is it wrong for a member to make no, or a token, contribution?

If the answers to these questions are yes, do we sense any obligation and responsibility to help everyone minister according to his God-given gift?

Is it wrong for church leaders to permit noninvolvement? If so, what should we do about it?

If every member is not involved in at least one ministry, we will not develop an ever-increasing leadership base to handle an increasing mass of people. A movement grows only as leadership is developed. The great problem in the church today is an inadequate base of qualified, committed leadership. Believers have to be cared for and serviced. If leadership is not being developed to provide the service, growth stops.

Even small churches need great amounts of involvement to function because the needs are so numerous and diverse. A growing church has an insatiable appetite for leadership. This is a constant struggle in our church. When we think we have enough leaders, we need twenty more nursery workers, teachers, or ushers. Unless all members are involved in ministry, there is no chance for growth. A small number of involved people cannot handle the demands.

If noninvolvement or token involvement persists, the effect on climate is negative. Noninvolvement, as we have mentioned before, destroys unity. The people who are involved soon become critical and bitter because they see themselves making all the commitments, sacrifices, and risks while everyone else receives the benefits.

One of the authors spoke about this subject in a morning service and afterward a woman called to say that she had developed critical attitudes toward some people whom she considered to be unfaithful and uncommitted in her particular area of ministry. She went to the people, apologized, and saw the people become more involved. How many people have harbored critical attitudes toward a brother or sister for this same reason? When unity is replaced by competition, hard feelings, criticism, and bitterness, the church is indeed ill. An uninvolved laity leads to the disease of disunity.

Ways to Stimulate Lay Involvement

We turn now to some practical ways in which leaders can stimulate lay people to be active in ministry.

Teach about Spiritual Gifts

People need to be taught and reminded about the biblical imperative of using their God-given abilities. They must see that it is a biblical issue. They must see themselves as stewards of their gifts in the same way that they see themselves stewards of their money. It is not an issue between themselves and the pastor. It is an issue between themselves and the Lord.

Teaching about spiritual gifts needs to be put in perspective. Too often, we have seen teaching about gifts which is so technical and systematized that it is confusing. We have seen unbelievably complex definitions of individual gifts. People unsuccessfully try to decide if and how they fit the definitions. This kind of confusion is unhealthy. People are confused and then become discouraged. At a retreat, one pastor began to challenge people to exercise their spiritual gifts. He had all those who knew their gifts stand. Then he asked all who did not know to stand. Some stood, embarrassed. The pastor smiled as if the exercise had accomplished something, but it only reconfirmed the guilt of "not knowing."

The truth is that it is hard to identify a spiritual gift. The New Testament does not give us the kind of definitions that many expositors use. The point is that sometimes we have taught a great deal about spiritual gifts and the teaching produces only confusion.

Several things are important in seeking to create a climate of involvement in ministry. Leaders should do four things.

Teach what the Scripture teaches. Seek to be flexible enough that people can get an idea about what their gifts might be.

Give people an opportunity to minister. Trying to have an uninvolved person determine what his gift is is generally a waste of time. Spiritual gifts are discerned and confirmed by involvement.

Encourage people to discern how their ministries affect others. Other people can confirm if a person does indeed have a particular gift.

Encourage people to express their likes and dislikes. What motivates them? Are they fulfilled by relationships with other people, by meeting objectives, by production? People need to know themselves.

We need to do more teaching about involvement but need to do it in a practical manner. After people have been ministering for a time and have seen response to their ministries, they are in a position to accurately identify their spiritual gifts. The only reason for a person to try to identify his or her gift is to confirm the focus of ministry. This helps to guide a person into a fruitful, fulfilling area of service. For example, if I am gifted in service, I should not try to be an administrator. I should concentrate my efforts. Knowing my gifts helps me to do that.

Survey Interests and Skills

One helpful way to begin to design a system for recruiting and involvement is to take a survey of the interests and skills of individuals within a congregation. We have listed all of our church ministries and potential involvements in a four-page form. We ask people to read the form and check the specific areas of ministry which interest them. The responses are then recorded on a coded card and used in recruiting for various ministries.

The advantage of a survey is that you can match a person with a task that interests him. This process may indicate his spiritual gift. Performing a job that he enjoys and is interested in is infinitely more fulfilling than performing one that he has no interest in. Whenever we talk to a new person in our church we always ask what (if anything) he has done before in churches, and what he likes to do.

In this regard, do not be afraid of people moving from job to job in a church. We have observed that sometimes people move around quite a bit before they settle into jobs which correspond to their gifts. This is a process of experimentation and can be healthy. We have several people at any given time in our church who are the wrong people for a particular job. They have not found their places yet. But they will. When they do find their places, they and you will know that it is right. This point is crucial. Recruiting people to things they like to do saves time in motivation and supervision. It creates a climate for growth.

Use Membership Classes to Emphasize Commitment

Membership classes can be tools for explaining expectations about involvement. We use the classes to talk about the philosophy, purpose, organizational structure, and internal-ministry structure of the church. In some churches, membership classes resemble classes in systematic theology. But people need to know what the church does, what its philosophy is, and how they fit into the church. Membership classes provide a platform to emphasize commitment and involvement. People are saying, by being there, that they want to commit themselves to you. To use this opportunity to teach theology may not be the wisest use of this time. Membership classes provide a special opportunity to talk about commitment. People are receptive to new ideas at this time. For example, we tell our people in these classes that they are expected, because of the biblical mandate, to be involved in one ministry in the church.

Analyze Involvement of Present Members

One problem that many church members have is a fuzzy, incomplete picture of the workload and the work force in the church. This is part of the diagnostic work that needs to be done in every church.

Find out how many members and people who attend regularly are presently involved in at least one ministry. What percentage is this of your total membership and/or adult attendance? If it is less than 80 percent, you probably have an overburdened and disgruntled group of workers.

What is the distribution of the workload? What percentage of workers is involved in work which is focused primarily within the body (e.g., teaching or ushering)? What percentage of workers is involved in work which is focused primarily outside the body?

What is the approximate amount of time spent on ministry? The average strong commitment will be five or six hours per week, excluding the regular services of the church.

One way to gather this kind of information is to design a survey and have your leaders answer the questions. We did this in our church and were surprised at how many people were involved in more than one ministry and how many were spending as much as twenty hours a week in ministry. The results showed us that our workload was not well distributed and that our work force was too small. If this is the case, it is an indication that you are headed for trouble if you do not deal with the inequities.

Recruit Properly

Most pastors and church leaders are not good delegators and recruiters. Several things need to be kept in mind.

Recruit people for one major ministry. Most laymen do not have time to do more than one thing well. Some pastors have asked what to do if there are not enough people, and leaders have to do more than one thing. Obviously this will happen. The whole workload and work force have to be studied. Does the ministry have to be done and done now? Are there uninvolved people who could do more if challenged and motivated? If God wants the work to be done and done now, He has people to do it. It would be better to postpone or discontinue a ministry than to overwork the committed leaders. That group is a precious asset. Sometimes the additional work is not worth the resulting disunity and burden.

Make sure the expectations are the same. This requires job descriptions which, in the simplest form, merely list the responsibilities involved in the job. It is appalling how many pastors work without job descriptions. How many people in the church really understand what is expected of them when they are recruited for a job? Not only is it necessary to have common expectations, but the person also needs to know to whom he is accountable and what budget he is working within. Common expectations are important because without them only frustration can result. Without clear expectations no meaningful evaluation or control can occur. The problem contributes to a negative climate in the church because the impression is that the church is mismanaged and imcompetent.

Build control factors into the recruiting process. If at all possible, put a time limit on the involvement. At the agreed-on time, mutual evaluation will take place and the desirability of continued involvement will be decided. Checkpoints to evaluate progress against objectives must be built into the process. Ask, "How are we doing (against agreed-on objectives)? What do we need to do this week or this month?" These questions will help people to see and accept accountability.

Train Lay People to Recruit Others

It is a good idea to have laymen recruit laymen, whenever possible. This communicates lay involvement in a way that the pastor could never duplicate. Laymen can enlist people. We allow the people in charge of our lay ministry to do much of the churchwide recruiting. The staff needs to provide names of potential workers because they have access to and know more names, but the laymen can recruit if given a chance.

The Impact of Lay Involvement

Lay involvement will affect quantitative growth because as the workload is evenly distributed, more people can be serviced, a greater variety of needs met, and more ministries provided. The church will be active instead of passive. There will be an excitement which will affect the attractiveness of the church and its magnetic power.

Qualitatively the body will be built up, in the language of Ephesians 4:16, "by that which every joint supplies." People will be fulfilled. Leaders will not have to coerce members into ministering. The counseling load will decrease because people will be busy and they will think about others instead of themselves.

Organically, the leaders will benefit if a steady stream of people are being involved in ministry. People will not be overworked. Positions will be filled. Training will take place and leaders will be fulfilled.

Action Items

How many people in your church are active in the ministry of evangelism and then of edification? Is only a small percentage of your membership involved?

How many people have more than one major ministry?

This chapter lists six ways to stimulate lay involvement. Which one does your church tend to fail in?

Suggest steps to strengthen these weak areas.

Bibliography

Arn, Wynn. *Advanced Seminars on Church Growth*. Pasadena, CA: American Institute of Church Growth, 1976.

MacArthur, John, Jr. *The Church: The Body of Christ*. Grand Rapids: Zondervan, 1973.

Stedman, Ray C. *Body Life*. Revised edition. Glendale, CA: Regal, 1979.

Western Conservative Baptist Seminary. *Spiritual Gifts Inventory*. Portland, OR.

Yohn, Rick. *Discover Your Spiritual Gift and Use It*. Wheaton, IL: Tyndale, 1975.

11

Absorption

We have discussed the characteristics that make a church attractive to people in the community. We turn now to a consideration of the principle of absorption. In John 15:16 Jesus tells us that He chose us to "... go and bear fruit—fruit that will last." Evangelism provides a constant flow of new converts and potential disciples. These new disciples must be effectively incorporated into the life of the body and into its discipling activities. An attitude and structure must exist in the church so new people can be easily absorbed into its life.

As our physical body has a process (digestion) for absorbing the nutrients from our food to produce health and growth, so the church needs a process (absorption) by which people can effectively experience its life.

Absorption Defined

We define absorption as the process by which people are taken into the life of the church and by which a strong sense of identity and belonging develops.

Assimilation occurs when a person develops a strong sense of identity with the church. A person must sense that he belongs here and that he is comfortable with the teaching, organization, goals, and purpose of the church. The growth of the church depends on how quickly the new disciple and the church cohere.

Absorption Described

Whether a person becomes part of a congregation depends on the attitude and structure of the church. This also depends on whether absorption is an easy and identifiable process. One indication of this is the length of time between the first visit and the application for membership and complete commitment to the church. The assimilation process involves what goes on between those two points. Another indication is the length of time it takes the new person to begin to refer to the church as "my" church instead of "your" church. Church growth will depend on how quickly that person makes a commitment to the church's life and work. This commitment will depend on the degree to which the person identifies with the church and the degree to which he feels that he belongs there.

Effective absorption will depend on how easy it is to become part of a congregation. By this we mean forming working relationships with people, visiting in their homes, understanding their joys, frustrations, and dreams. This is difficult under the best of circumstances. It is never easy to join a new group. Two major problems hinder the ease of entry into the church.

The first barrier is attitude. This is a more serious problem than most of us want to admit. In many churches, those who already belong do not want anyone else to join. These people fear growth. They fear that if new people continue to come, the intimacy and fellowship of the group will be destroyed. They equate smallness with intimacy and friendliness, which everyone needs. But new people mean change in one degree or another. To speak of growth is to speak of change. Growth implies a loss of intimacy. So we give lip service to growth and outreach, but we do not want the church to grow.

A new person can sense this attitude. He goes to a Sunday-school class, tries to join the choir or other organization in the church, and tries in other ways to participate in the life of the body. But he senses that the door is closed. He senses that people do not care if he stays. Soon he makes his way out of the church to another church where he can "get in." Needless to say, this church will never increase except by biological growth.

People have to see that if the assimilation process works in the right way it is possible to be a part of a large church and still experience an intimate relationship and strong identity with the body.

A second problem which slows absorption is the lack of an identifiable way to assimilate new people. There must be a process by which people can be contacted and invited to appropriate activities within the body. Are people quickly contacted and welcomed to the church after an initial visit? When a person evidences a genuine interest in the church is it easy for him and/or his family to be involved? Many churches are not prepared to involve new people. There is no procedure by which Sunday-school teachers, Bible-study leaders, or children's workers receive names of new people. Establishing such a process will not guarantee involvement (because some will not want to be involved), but it will make a powerful statement about our attitude. It will say, "We want you!"

We constantly give the names of people who regularly attend our church to the people who are in charge of various ministries. These people take the names and contact the new people. The people in charge of the ministries make the assimilation process work. They involve new people in fellowship and service activities. For example, we want to be sure that our home Bible-study leaders contact the visitors and potential new members in their geographical area to invite those new people to their group. We want this invitation to be made promptly and genuinely. We want to make it as easy as possible for someone to get involved in growth and service activities if he wants to.

Absorption Developed

We have defined effective absorption and have described barriers to assimilation. We now want to discuss specific activities or programs that aid assimilation.

You will remember that we earlier discussed the three strata in a healthy church. Usually a person first comes into contact with the church through the worship service (celebration). Celebration does not provide a sense of belonging or identity. Smaller groups are necessary if these needs are to be met. These two qualities—identity and sense of belonging—begin to be developed on the subcongregational level.

Subcongregations include three types of groups: Sunday-school classes; age-level ministry groups (e.g., high school, junior high, singles, or elderly); service groups (e.g., choirs or missionary organizations). The size of these groups (from 40 to 110 people) makes them valuable in assimilating new people. These groups are large enough to be low-commitment groups but small enough to allow a newcomer to know some people on a first-name basis. Knowing first names is the first step toward a sense of belonging. It eliminates the strangeness. It helps provide a feeling of acceptance. In our church, newcomers are invited to join these groups. The adult Sunday-school classes are the first places that begin to help newcomers assimilate.

Subcongregations are vital to the assimilation process because they meet the needs of identity and belonging. They do this in three ways.

Social Relationship

Social relationships begin here. The Sunday-school class can meet social needs, because in it people begin to feel welcome. A wise adult Sunday-school leader will schedule regular social activities for his class. If people meet in each other's homes and do amusing things together, they will feel a sense of belonging and identity. Even identity groups that are service-oriented (for example, the choir) will want to have regularly-scheduled social activities.

People want and need to enjoy the company of another person or group of people. Social activities begin to meet this need. They begin to gradually integrate people into the group. They provide a sense of belonging, and a climate for growth and involvement. They whet the appetite for more involvement, and hence are a way to assimilate newcomers.

Internal Structure

The second thing about subcongregations which makes them channels for absorbing newcomers is their internal structure. There is an identifiable leadership and activity structure with presidents, leaders, committees, and budgets. People identify with a specific entity within the larger church. People can identify this group as "my group." This is important in a growing church. The subcongregation, with its specific structure of responsibility, can provide a way to fit in. We like to hear statements which begin with, "In my class, or groups, we do. . . . " These statements show identification with an entity.

If a church is to grow, it must decentralize. It must expand its ministry to the subcongregations. The internal structure of the groups gives leadership a chance to develop. Responsibility at this level furthers the sense of belonging. To be on a committee or to be an officer in a class or group develops commitment to the group and also to the church. We try to get as many people as possible involved in these groups in some way, even minimally. The involvement in tasks related to the group furthers identity with the group.

The social structure of a subcongregation helps provide a sense of belonging, but other projects and activities can be done by a class or group. Whatever can be done as a group—specific missionary projects, giving, or work days—helps develop a healthy loyalty and commitment to a group.

This commitment to and identity with a subcongregation provides an answer to the fear about a big church. No matter what the size of a church, a person can know only a certain number of people and establish only a certain number of close relationships. It does not matter whether a church has two hundred or five thousand members. Unless a church has only one hundred or fewer people, there is no chance of knowing everyone. In a larger church, the secret is to quickly absorb people into subcongregations as a structure for meeting people. Sitting in a large Sunday morning service with no other involvement will become very discouraging unless a person is deliberately seeking anonymity.

Caring and Shepherding

The third thing which provides a sense of belonging is that caring and shepherding begin to occur within subcongregations. If the internal structure of the group is adequate, people will notice when others are absent. This is a barometer of whether people feel accepted: "Does anyone notice when I'm not there, and if so, does anyone care?" Nothing is as satisfying as the simple comment, "We missed you."

At this level, people can tell others about sickness, family crises, or financial difficulty. Together they can pray about these needs. People can offer practical assistance. These needs cannot be met at the celebration level. A structure must exist to let these needs be known and to meet them; on this level that can occur.

Due to the size of a subcongregation, we must not expect that deep relationships will develop here. Smaller groups (cells) are necessary for this to occur. People will form stronger relationships as they join smaller groups and become more heavily committed to ministry. The subcongregation is the first level where people begin to sense that "this is my group and my church." You should expect people, after a while, to seek out more in-depth involvement in smaller groups and ministry opportunities. They may and probably will stay in their subcongregations, but they have other needs that cannot be met here.

Absorption Diagnosed

Since the subcongregational level of involvement is so important, any church which wants to grow should regularly diagnose its subcongegations. There are three basic steps in this process.

Analyze the Need

Church leaders need to understand the contribution that a strong network of subcongregations makes to the whole body. For some churches this may involve a different definition of "church." Most people define "church" as celebration. "Did you go to church today?" means, "Did you go to the Sunday morning worship service?" The New Testament does not endorse such a definition, because the New Testament emphasizes ministry to and with one another. Celebration meets the need for corporate worship, but it cannot provide involvement in each other's lives.

Many churches not only ignore the need for these various involvement levels but also are actually afraid to meet needs. We must see that growth depends on developing strong subcongregations. Not to do so ignores the basic human need for social interaction and the basic spiritual need for deep fellowship and ministry to one another.

Analyze the need biblically and philosophically. A pastor should do an in-depth study of all the appropriate New Testament passages, and then discuss creative ways to involve people in these ministries. We soon would not discuss the Sunday morning worship but the need for smaller groups. Whatever state these groups are in presently, diagnose the effectiveness and degree of assimilation that these groups provide the church.

Create a Thirst

Probably a thirst already exists for fellowship and relationships, but a church needs to keep these groups and their functions before the people. Highlight the biblical mandate for developing relationships or the spiritual value and benefit of fellowship. Realize that most people define church in celebration terms. Thirst is also created by testimonies. Our adult Sunday school increased substantially after we had two people speak about "what Sunday school means to me" during six consecutive Sunday morning services. Personal experience of the benefits of any program will stimulate interest and attention.

Develop Leadership

One of the greatest needs in the church is for leadership at the subcongregational level. Subcongregations require a whole leadership structure. An adult Sunday-school class not only needs an excellent teacher but also a group of committed leaders who will handle the shepherding, social activities, finances, and class leadership. We try to structure our classes in such a way that the teacher does not have to do everything. His main function is teaching.

A subcongregation which is not a class will soon see the need to involve many people in responsible work. This is healthy in and of itself. It contributes to the church's ability to assimilate new people. As we have already said, involving people in ministry, however minimal, is in itself a way to create a sense of belonging and identity.

Relationship to Church Growth

Quantitative growth will be directly affected by the degree to which a church can absorb new people into its fellowship and life. Some people will not feel a compatibility with the group. A church will not be able to meet the special needs of everyone. But ease of absorption will allow us to retain a greater number of people and will thus affect numerical growth.

Qualitative growth will be affected by this principle because the ministry of the body will be decentralized. There will be a healthier awareness of the need to minister to one another. Relationships will be initiated. People will begin to meet each other's needs and not look to the celebration to meet all of the spiritual needs. A strong internal commitment will develop as people develop an identity with the body. People will begin to acknowledge goals as they begin to think in terms of "my" and "our" instead of "your." Membership will increase significantly. A strong involvement in a subcongregation will shorten the time between the initial contact and membership; increased membership will mean increased giving, involvement in ministry, and leadership potential.

Organic growth will be greatly influenced by the degree of absorption. The subcongregations will provide potential leaders. As people develop a sense of identity and commitment, they will be available for leadership. The work force will increase, and a church always needs workers.

Action Items

Evaluate your church's ability to absorb new people. Does your church have the right social relationships and social structure to allow for absorption?

Diagnose your church's process of absorption, using the principles given in this chapter.

Suggest specific ways to improve that process.

Bibliography

Getz, Gene A. *The Measure of a Church*. Glendale, CA: Regal, 1975.

MacArthur, John, Jr. *The Church: The Body of Christ*. Grand Rapids: Zondervan, 1973.

Schaller, Lyle E. *Assimilating New Members*. Nashville: Abingdon, 1978.

Wagner, C. Peter. *Your Church Can Grow*. Glendale: CA: Regal, 1976.

12

Small Groups

In earlier chapters, we defined and discussed the celebration and the subcongregation. In this chapter, we will discuss the third level in a healthy church—the small group, or cell.

The small group represents a more advanced stage of assimilation or absorption than does the subcongregation. The cell differs from the subcongregation in three important ways.

The first of these differences is size. The cell is ideally limited to 3 to 10 people. As we saw in the last chapter, the subcongregation can range from 40 to 110 people. The difference in size reflects the second difference.

This second difference is function. The subcongregation is organized to stimulate a sense of belonging and identity. It is intended to be the first stage of the absorption process. The cell, on the other hand, allows deeper commitment and involvement. Its primary functions are intimacy and accountability. We will define these twin needs later.

The third difference is makeup. The subcongregation will generally be heterogeneous, (i.e., include people of different ages, backgrounds, and sex). The participants do not have to be generally alike to function together in the group. Conversely, the cell (in our opinion) functions best when it is homogeneous—made up of people who are alike with respect to age and sex.

Purpose of the Small Group

We first want to consider the purpose of the cell or small group. That purpose is to develop deep interpersonal relationships. As we have said, the subcongregation begins this process through social activities and basic leadership development. The small group provides an opportunity to develop the fuller range of relationships that the New Testament exhorts us to develop.

We need to consider three things about building relationships in the church context.

Self-Image

The basis for developing strong interpersonal relationships is a biblically healthy self-image. I will not be free to love another person and focus on the other person's needs unless I am seeing myself as God sees me and until I am secure in His love and acceptance. If I am to have a positive self-image and thus be free to love others, I must realize that God has made me the way I am for a purpose. I can be thankful for three things.

I am uniquely made. Psalm 139 is a beautiful expression of the inestimable value that God places on me. I am physically unique, mentally unique, and have a unique personality.

I have unique abilities. I have a unique combination of natural gifts and abilities, spiritual gifts, and developed talents. I can do things that no one else in the whole world can do.

I have a unique background. I have a national inheritance, racial background, and family which are unique to me. Educationally and socially I am also special. I can minister uniquely to others out of my background in a way that no one else can.

God has sovereignly designed me by physical, mental, and psychological makeup, and by background, to fulfill in and through me His special purposes for my life. Nothing about me has developed or come about by mistake. In light of God's creative purpose in my life I am free to love others totally because I am secure in His acceptance.

Attitude

The second essential thing about building relationships is the attitude needed to relate properly to others. This attitude springs from a positive self-image. We need to accept the fact that there are differences in the way God made us and in His purpose for our lives. We need to thank God for our common relationship to Christ and also for our differences.

One of the great problems in the family and the church today is the failure to let other people be different from us. For example, our children are not like us. God has made then unique. Their tastes are not precisely like ours. They need to be free to develop their uniquenesses. The same is true in the body of Christ. All of us come from different backgrounds, churches, and lifestyles. We must appreciate the way God is uniquely working in a brother's life and not always try to shape him into our image. Legalism forces our likes and standards onto someone else and equates our standards with God's standards. But the church does not exist to make carbon copies of anyone except Jesus Christ. The route to Christ-likeness will be unique to every person. We need to recognize and accept the healthy diversity of the body of Christ. I Corinthians 12:4– 6 makes this clear.

> There are *different kinds of gifts*, but the same Spirit.
> There are *different kinds of service*, but the same Lord.
> There are *different kinds of working*, but the same God works all of them in all men. (italics ours)

The constant factor in all of our relationships and ministry is the Lord. The variety of gifts, ministries, and results within a local body of believers is astounding.

God not only created each of us in a unique way to perform a unique function, but He also created everyone else to be unique and to perform a unique ministry. Many problems within the church spring from a lack of appreciation for the other person and his or her differences from us.

Toleration is needed nowhere more than in a church leadership group. Every member comes from a different church background, has different gifts, is motivated by different things, and approaches problems in different ways. A lack of understanding of and appreciation for this fact creates problems. The tolerance level is low and patience is tried. If we expect everyone to start and come out at the same place on every issue we will be constantly frustrated. God did not create us that way. We need to learn how to hold strong personal convictions and at the same time appreciate others' views and learn how God will use someone else's life to influence our lives. The strength of the body lies in the unity that God builds in spite of the diversity.

Biblical Principles

The third thing to consider is that several basic principles from the New Testament will help to define and direct the development of relationships in small groups. Small groups are not ends in themselves. They are the means to achieve strong relationships within the body. Remember that herein lies the attracting power of the church. Nonmembers will be drawn to visible love relationships.

A much-overlooked principle of New Testament ministry is that, in the context of the church, *every* believer is a minister. Today we often think that the pastor and other full-time workers are responsible for ministry. Lay people are the passive spectators and can do "jobs" in the church, but the "minister" ministers. This attitude is unbiblical and constitutes a disease which threatens the whole health of the body. In our church bulletin the section which lists the church staff begins with these words:

Ministers: Every Member

The New Testament teaches that believers must minister to each other. The pattern is not to come, to sit, and to be taught. There is a need for a gifted man to unfold the meaning of the Word. But every believer is to participate. We do not only have someone minister to us, but we also minister to and with others.

A second principle defines the way in which we minister to and with one another: It is through the full range of the "one another" ministries of the New Testament. Love encompasses all of these ministries. These expressions, and they are numerous, are not practiced only by the full-time ministers, but also by every believer. We are told to:

Comfort one another	I Thessalonians 4:18
Encourage one another	I Thessalonians 5:11
Build up one another	I Thessalonians 5:11
Live in peace with one another	I Thessalonians 5:13
Seek what is good for one another	I Thessalonians 5:13
Stimulate one another	Hebrews 10:24
Confess sins to one another	James 5:16
Pray for one another	James 5:16

Not complain against one another	James 5:9
Not judge one another	Romans 14:13
Not consume or devour one another	Galatians 5:15
Offer hospitality to one another	I Peter 4:9
Prefer one another	Romans 12:10
Edify one another	Romans 14:19
Receive one another	Romans 15:7
Admonish one another	Romans 15:14
Care for one another	I Corinthians 12:25
Greet one another	I Corinthians 16:20
Serve one another	Galatians 5:13
Submit to one another	Ephesians 5:21

This is only a sample of attitudes and actions that Christians should exhibit. For too long we have defined the church in terms of Sunday morning worship. But we cannot truly minister to one another on the congregational level. These ministries must be carried on in smaller groups of people. In-depth relationships depend on these ministries. There must be a balance in our teaching, as there is in the New Testament, between doctrine and the development of godly characteristics. For the latter to be so prominent in the New Testament and so lacking in modern preaching may show why so many churches have beautifully correct doctrinal statements and believe all the right things but are divided. Correct doctrine rarely attracts someone to a church. It is important to believe the right things, but the New Testament beautifully balances doctrine with teaching about how we should behave toward each other.

Functions of the Small Group

With these principles as the background, we turn now to examining the small group itself. The small group is the primary method through which the believers can minister to each other. The celebration cannot meet this need. The subcongregation helps people to begin to establish friendships, but it is in the small group that in-depth relationships are formed. The small group has three functions.

Intimacy

The first function is the development of intimacy. Intimacy is a greatly misunderstood and greatly feared word, because most people have never experienced a genuine spiritual intimacy with a group of fellow believers. The word *intimacy* is associated with the encounter-group experience in which a person is encouraged to tell all of his problems. Spiritual intimacy, developed in the small group, is not an encounter-group experience. It is not a gossip session. It is not programmed, manufactured, or forced.

Intimacy develops in time, by the structure of the group itself and what goes on in it. Members of small groups do two things.

The first ingredient is the study of the Scripture. The Scripture is central to the purpose of the small group. It is central to the development of relationships. Colossians 3:16 tells us to "Let the Word of Christ dwell in you richly as you teach and admonish one another with all wisdom. . . ."

In small groups, studying the Bible is not merely an academic exercise. It is not a way to accumulate additional factual information, although that will happen. But the purpose is to study Scripture and apply its truths to our lives.

People in small groups will tell each other about their problems, and this is healthy if it is in response to Scripture. Otherwise the discussion can degenerate into gossip or a maudlin account about one's problems.

All of us need to learn to stimulate and encourage one another (Heb. 10:24–25). The main way we can do this is by studying the Word or explaining how the Word was and is being used in our experiences. For example, it is encouraging to say, "I know what you're experiencing. When I was going through a similar situation, the Lord directed me to this passage. Let's study it together."

Many churches are afraid of not being able to control small groups. Churches fear heresy will develop. The way to control the groups is the recruitment and training of qualified leaders, and part of the training includes how to keep discussion and personal comments focused on response to the Word. The content of the passage being studied will trigger response and personal reaction to it.

This response to Scripture will develop a healthy intimacy. The focus will be on what God is teaching us individually and collectively. It is natural to apply those teachings to our lives, and personal comments will relate to how we responded and are responding to the Word.

Many formats and materials are available for small-group Bible study. We caution readers that sometimes Christians fall into the pattern of studying all kinds of material about the Bible and others' opinions about the meaning of Scripture, but never study the Word itself. The practical sections of the Epistles will provide much to study and are a good place to start. Also, the general Epistles are useful for a group's Bible study.

The second ingredient of a small-group meeting is prayer. Prayer for one another's needs is a beautiful way to develop healthy intimacy. Do not try to force people to talk about personal problems. The willingness to share needs will develop as a love/trust relationship develops in the group and as God speaks to us through the Word. Many times, in small groups, we have heard comments such as, "Tonight as we were studying this passage God spoke to me and I'm convicted about.... Pray for me in this area." The requests for prayer flow from the study of Scripture. If the members of a group are reluctant to talk about things of a personal nature, do not force them to do so. Let the Lord develop that desire and willingness. Beautiful relationships will develop as people come together to pray and then share answers to prayer.

As both of these things happen the by-products will be a healthy willingness to discuss personal matters and a deepening fellowship. The focus on the Lord and the Word will keep the groups healthy. Another by-product will be growth of the individuals.

Accountability

The second function of a small group is accountability. The beautiful internal quality of a small group is the accountability that eventually develops. Part of the problem in church life is that there is not the healthy challenge from others to do the things we know we should do. For example, we started a men's Bible-study group two years ago. One of the things we wanted to do was memorize Scripture together. Several men were reluctant at first but we assigned the first two verses. The next week only two men had memorized them. Those men said the verses, and we assigned two more verses. Soon, everybody was memorizing the verses and it was not due to external pressure. The men saw their brothers doing it and the healthy pressure of example created a desire in them to do it as well. Proverbs 27:17 emphasizes this: "As iron sharpens iron, so one man sharpens another."

We have seen this principle at work in many different situations, especially in small groups. For example, a group of women who struggle with obesity meet to pray, study the Word, and encourage one another in their attempts to deal with this problem. It works because of the healthy pressure.

Hebrews 13:17 exhorts the members of a body to "obey your leaders and submit to their authority. They keep watch over you as men who must give an account." There is a natural accountability in the body. God has given us leaders to whom we are to submit. They are to be held accountable for their watch over our souls. In the small-group context the accountability is mutual. All of us need it. We need to be challenged by others. All of us know we should have times alone with the Lord, memorize Scripture, and do other things, but it is so easy not to. In a small group it is easier to do what we should because others are also doing these things. This stimulates others to faithfulness. Real growth occurs in a life when healthy accountability is present. The small group is the ideal place for this quality to develop.

Most pastors are not accountable to anyone. They need this as much, if not more, than anyone else. A healthy by-product of the Christian Leadership Training Center for pastors is the accountability that develops among the men. Such accountability is the "iron sharpening iron" principle in action.

Stimulation and Encouragement

A third function—which is a by-product of intimacy and accountability—is the practice of stimulating and encouraging one another. These particular expressions are found in Hebrews 10:24–25 (NASB), which says, "... and let us consider how to stimulate one another to love and good deeds, not forsaking our own assembling together, as is the habit of some, but encouraging one another...."

We are exhorted to practice these two ministries in the context of the small group (assembling together). Something about being together with those who share a relationship to Christ is uniquely stimulating and encouraging. We are told to "consider" how to stimulate and encourage. Why is this a need? Why should we reflect on how to do it?

The small group is uniquely equipped to meet two specific needs that relate to encouragement.

The first need for encouragement is in the area of perseverance. Hebrews, Peter's epistles, and other New Testament writings attest to the external pressures on the faith and commitment of believers. Jesus, in John 15, explains to the disciples that the world will hate them and persecute them. Today we face those pressures as well as crisis situations and mental and emotional strain. We need to be able to come into the oasis of a warm, supportive group of brothers and sisters to be encouraged to persevere—to be ministered to by the Word and the experience of others.

The second need for stimulation and encouragement is in the area of behavior. We come into the body of Christ with baggage from the old way of life. The goal of the Christian walk is Christ-likeness in behavior and character. We are constantly confronted with the need to "put off" certain behavior and "put on" other behavior. A supportive, encouraging relationship with a small group can be powerful in keeping us motivated to please God in all our behavior. It is easy to lose the motivation. The Christian life is a struggle and a war (Rom. 6; Gal. 5). It is easy to give in to pressure to continue in ungodly habits and thoughts. We are dependent only on God and His Spirit for power and resource, but God uses the encouragement of the brothers and sisters to motivate us to continue to yield unyielded areas of behavior and character to Him.

These are the functions of the small group. Those functions cannot be provided in-depth anywhere else. We covet for everyone in our church the beautiful intimacy of a small-group relationship. It is priceless.

Small groups should be seen in relation to subcongregations. These represent two levels of involvement. A church needs to develop its subcongregational level first. It is difficult to move from the celebration to the cell. The cell demands more commitment and accountability than the subcongregation does. When the church has a healthy subcongregational level, it has provided an effective way for people to fully assimilate into the church. New people will gravitate to an adult Sunday-school class before they will to a small group.

Small groups are of infinite variety. Some spring from evangelistic Bible studies. Some are groups of couples. Others are made up of men or women. Some are informal, unstructured prayer groups. Some come out of church subcongregations. Others are structured, limited in membership, and focused on in-depth technical discipleship and study. It is difficult to describe an ideal group. Groups come in all different forms. Whatever the form, the small group is essential in carrying out the "one another" relationships described in the New Testament.

The principles we have discussed in this chapter apply to functional groups within the church which are not normally thought of as small groups. Every church has governing bodies (elders and deacons), committees, leadership groups within the church, and other kinds of functional groups. Although their purpose is not the same as that of a Bible-study or cell group, the same principles of ministry and prayer apply. In fact, sometimes these functional groups surpass the others in terms of intimacy and encouragement because of the commonality of the members' involvement and commitment.

Impact of Small Groups on Church Growth

There is tremendous impetus for church growth in small groups, because the structure and functions of small groups encourage ministry.

Qualitative growth will be affected because of leadership development. Members will have close relationships with each other, resulting in personal growth. Members will minister to each other, and informally counsel each other.

The church with strong celebration, subcongregations, and small groups will experience the same relationships exhibited in the early church. Such relationships will be attractive to those outside the church's doors, and this provides for quantitative growth.

Small groups are *key* to organic growth, because their structure gives a basis for leadership development.

Action Items

Evaluate the structure of your church's small groups and the objectives of each group.

How effective are your church's members in ministering to one another? Go back and look at the "one another" passages listed in this chapter. Indicate the ones that need to be developed in your church.

Choose one of those weakest areas and determine how you would start to build that quality in your church, especially through activities in small groups.

Bibliography

Alexander, John W. *Practical Criticism: Giving and Receiving It*. Downers Grove, IL: Inter-Varsity, 1976.

Augsburger, David. *Caring Enough to Confront*. Revised edition. Glendale, CA: Regal, 1979.

Churches Alive. This consulting group advises churches about church growth, particularly as growth pertains to leadership and small groups. San Bernardino, CA.

Getz, Gene A. *Building Up One Another*. Wheaton, IL: Victor Books, 1976.

Jenson, Ronald. *How to Succeed the Biblical Way*. Wheaton, IL: Tyndale, 1981. See pp. 87–94.

Richards, Lawrence O. *A New Face for the Church*. Grand Rapids: Zondervan, 1970.

13

Discipleship

The principle of discipleship is crucial to understanding church health and growth. Discipleship is one of those foundational principles on which all the others rest, because it lies at the heart of the church's purpose. The local church is God's great method for fulfilling the Great Commission (Matt. 28:18–20), which is to "make disciples." Cut off from this purpose and product the church is at best a social organization.

Discipling makes church ministry and development exciting and stimulating. The church exists for nothing less than creating a different kind of people. The church has been designed by God with everything necessary to disciple people (i.e., develop them into Christ-likeness).

It is imperative that we understand the way in which the church makes disciples. The church is its own discipleship model. It has an internal organization, structure, and climate which blend together in a supernatural way to develop disciples.

In considering the principle of discipleship we must begin with definitions. Several well-known parachurch organizations emphasize discipleship. The definitions of "disciple" and "discipleship" imported into the church from these groups, although helpful, are inadequate to describe the way the church makes disciples. The church is uniquely equipped by God to disciple in a way that no other organization can duplicate.

The New Testament describes two types of discipleship and discipling activity. Discipling is done in a technical sense and in a corporate sense.

Technical Discipleship

Technical discipleship describes the intense concentration of attention on a man or small group of men for the purpose of spiritual growth and leadership development. Technical discipleship uses Christ's training methods — instruction, demonstration, involvement, and evaluation.

The focus in technical discipleship is on the one-to-one relationship or the one-to-three-or-four relationship (small group) of the one who makes disciples and those who learn. A person looks to another person for instruction, counsel, training, and fellowship.

Jesus practiced discipleship in this sense. He concentrated on selecting and developing a few men for the future leadership of the church. He lived with them, knew them intimately, and trained them personally. He selected twelve men, and in this small group narrowed His concentration to three who received special attention because of their future roles in the church.

Paul also practiced technical discipleship in his effort to develop church leaders. Throughout the Book of Acts and the Epistles we read of his intimate associations with Timothy, Titus, Luke, Silas, and others. Paul's instruction of Timothy is a particularly good example of an intense one-on-one discipling relationship. Paul's letters to him include personal exhortation and instruction, which no doubt was intensified in face-to-face discussion.

In order to understand technical discipleship and its relationship to corporate discipleship we need to understand the purpose of technical discipleship. Both Jesus and Paul were interested primarily in developing leaders. Jesus' plan for fulfilling the Great Commission was to train disciples who in turn would train other disciples. His primary focus was on developing the first generation of leadership. The whole process, which would operate through succeeding generations until His return, depended on that first generation.

Paul's focus (and that of the other apostles) was the development of the leadership for the early church. The apostles concentrated on the second generation of disciples. As the gospel message exploded throughout the first-century world, multitudes of new converts were harvested. That harvest had to be conserved, because the gospel had to be carried into the next generation. The formation of self-contained bodies (churches) of these new disciples was the answer to the conservation, maturation, and reproduction of this harvest. Leadership had to be developed for the church. Internal organization, structure, climate, absorption, and leadership were all issues which needed to be addressed. The apostles had to concentrate on developing that first generation of churches and the necessary leadership—thus Paul's concentration on the founding of churches, their development, and their leadership.

It is interesting that the word *disciple* does not occur in the Epistles. The reason is that in the Epistles, discipling is done, not on a one-to-one basis, but in the church. The church uniquely disciples. It practices corporate discipleship. The context of discipleship changes when we come to the Epistles. The emphasis is on the development of the body, rather than solely on the discipling of leaders.

Corporate Discipleship

Technical discipleship has a vital place in the church. Concentrating special attention on the church's leadership is necessary. We spend much personal time with our governing body, people in charge of ministries, and other leaders. The ministry depends on these people, so a ministry of personal encouragement, training, and discipling is essential. Although this kind of concentration on leadership is necessary, we do not believe that technical discipleship is the New Testament model for discipleship in its fullest sense. God has designed the internal climate and program of the church in such a way to disciple those who are exposed to and involved in the church.

God has initiated two processes in the local church which result in the discipling of its members. Without them, discipleship in the fullest sense cannot occur.

Exercise of Spiritual Gifts

The first process that God uses in the church is the exercise of spiritual gifts. In order for an individual to develop fully into Christlikeness, he needs the impact of a full range of spiritual gifts on his life. Technical discipleship alone cannot provide this because the person who disciples does not possess all the gifts. He can minister to another out of his particular uniqueness but the disciple needs the influence of the other gifts in his life. An individual can help another individual get started in the basics such as reading the Bible or memorizing Scripture, but discipleship in its fullest sense will occur in a corporate context. The church is the only place where the full expression of spiritual gifts can be found. Ephesians 4:16 tells us that the total body is built up and grows "as each part does its work." Every expression of a spiritual gift, whether it be teaching, service, administration, or any of the others, in some way ministers to a need that a new disciple has. The expression of all the gifts together provides the energy and climate for growth.

Ministry to One Another

The second process inherent in the local church is also one which cannot be duplicated outside the church. It is the full range of the "one another" expressions found in the Epistles. The new believer, in order to develop Christ-like behavior and character, needs the caring, exhorting, rebuking, praying, encouraging, and stimulating which other believers can provide in full measure in the church. In this context the body literally disciples itself. Discipleship is a corporate activity. In the church, all of us have incorporated parts of others' lives into our own lives. Discipling is not strictly a one-on-one process. Obviously personal attention is needed, but if the internal structure of the body is designed to include small-group and social activities, personal attention can be given and people ministered to and helped to grow.

Think of the potential. If every person were effectively ministering according to his or her spiritual gift and if all the "one another" ministries were occurring, discipleship would be taking place in the maximum way God intends it to take place. The church has every component necessary to produce disciples.

Most people, when discussing the need for and methodology of discipleship, think of discipleship primarily in the technical sense—that of one person spending time in discipling another person. From reading the Epistles, we know that this was done, but mostly with leadership. The primary focus was on the activity and internal function of the body.

As discipleship is occurring throughout the body, through its activities and its internal structure, life reproduces itself. There are two types of reproduction. First is reproduction in the evangelistic sense, which will occur through the attracting power of the body itself and through the ministry of those who are especially gifted in the work of evangelism. We think that every believer should know how to communicate his or her faith to another person. But not everyone will be involved in formal evangelism and the structured outreach program of the church.

Reproduction also occurs through the use of spiritual gifts. All believers will be involved in edification. For example, a teacher focuses on teaching. His contribution to the discipleship of people is teaching. The person with the gift of service will contribute to the discipleship of others by the faithful stewardship of that gift. Not everyone will do the same thing. Not everyone can do the same thing. We are all uniquely equipped by God to contribute to the discipleship of others.

The plans for world evangelization and discipleship in which one reaches and disciples one and that one reaches and disciples another are not realistic in and of themselves. After the number reaches twenty or so, some kind of organization is necessary. People need teachers, servers, and administrators. The focus of ministry ceases to be only the intense man-to-man activity and moves to the exercise of a gift for the corporate good.

The great need is for every believer to begin to minister to others in the area of his gift. We must not define discipleship and multiplication only as leading a person to Christ, doing basic follow-up, and/or leading a Bible-study group. It is a much broader process than that in the church because of the diversity of individual and family needs to be met. In II Timothy 2:2 Paul tells Timothy to pass on what he has heard from Paul to faithful men who could teach others. Paul is speaking to Timothy in a church context and is articulating a specific principle about the spiritual gift of teaching. He is not spelling out a general form or method of ministry.

Figure 3 shows the relationship of technical to body discipleship. Leaders (inner circle) are discipled through the training methods of Christ, the result of which is ministry in every area of church life—Sunday school, Bible studies, functional committees, youth, deacons, and others.

We are not saying that personal ministry has no place or that people do not need to be taught how to start the Christian life. We are saying that discipleship in the New Testament sense cannot be done on a one-to-one basis alone. The new disciple needs far more than a single person can give him. The church is the only way that a person can get all he

Figure 3

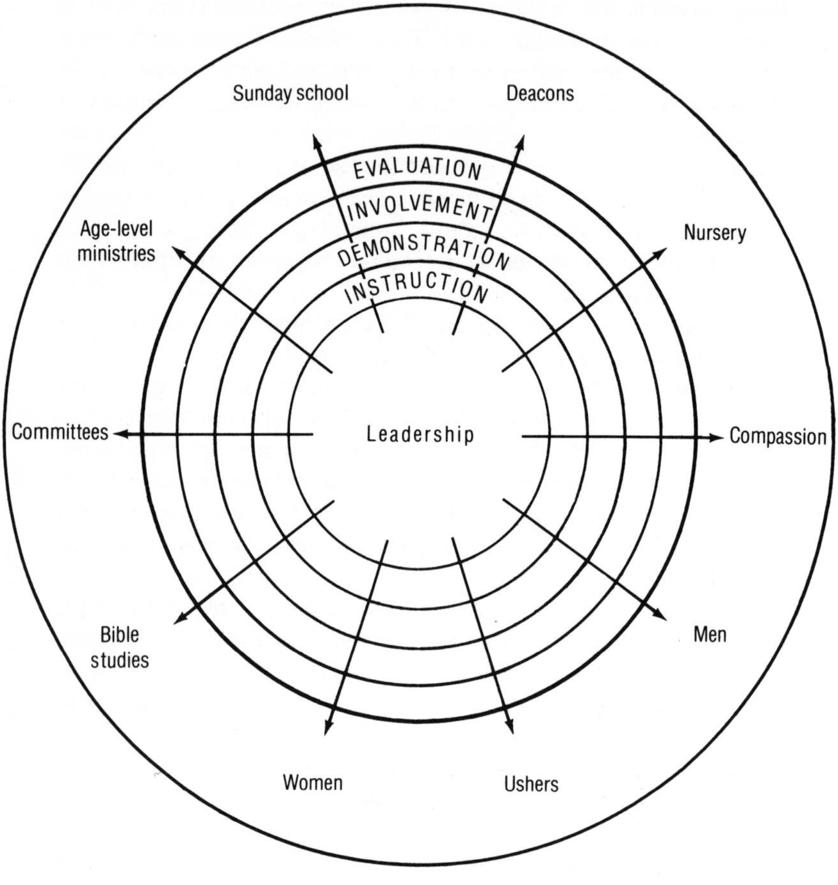

needs to develop Christ-likeness because God has built into the church the ways to accomplish the discipling purpose. Each believer needs to learn from others with various gifts and abilities.

Discipling Program or Discipling Church?

Does a church have a discipling program? In a strict methodological sense, no. The church has an internal structure which aims at meeting the spiritual and social needs of the disciple. Broadly speaking, everything that the church does contributes to the discipleship of its people. Every program and activity has as its purpose the development of people into committed disciples. That point is reached through the effect of the total church program and climate. A person comes to the church, is exposed to excellent teaching and music, is involved in a Sunday-school class and a small group, begins to minister to others according to his or her gift, develops strong interpersonal relationships where the "one another" ministries are exercised, is continually exposed to specific need-oriented instruction, learns by practice the godly habits of life, and is growing personally. At the same time the other family members are involved in the same process. The church provides for the family a climate and activites in which growth and ministry can occur in a maximum way.

This is a beautiful process to watch. We wish that we could trace the journey of every new believer through the church activities to see which needs are met at which places. If you can think of a person who came to Christ through your church and who is growing into a mature disciple, he probably is involved in your church on four levels. He is a regular participant in worship, he is in a vital Sunday-school class, he is in a small group, and he is involved in a ministry to others in the body. Specific needs are being met through reading, seminars, and practical instruction. He also has a vision to share his faith with others wherever and whenever possible.

The tragedy is that many new disciples are not involved in discipling churches. In order to grow they find themselves in discipling programs outside the church where they have to fit into the same mold as everyone else in the program. They cannot minister according to their gift or abilities and consequently are always searching for something more. The great need of our time is for discipling churches which will provide a climate for growth and opportunities for involvement in ministry.

Discipling Climate

In our chapter about climate we discussed several climate factors. Those factors apply in this discussion of discipleship but we would like to add several practical things here which serve to stimulate a desire to grow and minister.

Ultimately the desire to grow and progress in discipleship will depend on what God does in a person's life through exposure to God's truth. People who are learning the truth and how to apply it have a thirst for more. We need to emphasize excellent, practical, need-oriented teaching for every member of the body. Adult and age-level Sunday-school classes need excellent teaching. This "feeding ministry" would also include Bible studies, seminars, retreats, and other forums where people can study Scripture and its implications for their lives. The feeding ministry greatly enhances the climate in which discipleship takes place.

Matthew 18 and other passages give us the guidelines for dealing with known sin in the body. If a church is unwilling to deal with unforgiven sin, the climate for discipleship will be greatly affected. The consequences include bitterness, hard feelings, bad attitudes, and anger. In many churches it would be unheard of to discipline someone according to the process outlined in Matthew 18. We need to carefully study the way we handle interpersonal conflict within the body. God has given us His plan for handling it. He did so because He knew what devastation would be caused in the church if unresolved conflicts were allowed to fester. We spoke recently with a pastor who told us that it was difficult to get some of his people together for dinner because a number of them were not speaking to one another. When we asked how long this condition had existed, he replied, "For a long time." Another church is experiencing these kinds of conflicts between pastor and board. Leadership people are leaving, attendance and giving are declining, and the church will probably regroup in two or more factions. People are so preoccupied with these problems that assimilating new people is the last thing on their minds. Many of these problems stem from an unwillingness to follow the biblical guidelines for dealing with them. Pastors rarely preach about or teach from Matthew 18. One pastor said, "My people wouldn't stand for it!"

The greatest discipling potential lies in the family. To teach and encourage fathers to disciple their children would go a long way toward creating a climate for discipleship in the church. Many men and women are defeated in the church ministry because they are defeated at home. It is interesting that a qualification for church leadership (I Tim. 3; Titus 1) is the ability to manage the home. We need to give practical instruction about proper family roles and relationships to children, mothers, and fathers. Seminars, retreats, Sunday-school classes, and sermon series which are home-related are always well-attended in our church. Our men especially need to be helped in this area. They receive very little from the church. The discipling climate is enhanced when people know that we are committed to the family and home. Try a Saturday-morning series for men about "spiritual leadership in the home," or a retreat that deals with the same subject. Do not assume men know how to lead their families. Many men do not know the basic things about interpersonal relationships. They are afraid of their teen-age children. They do not know how to love their wives. Many a time we have seen men weep as they said, "If only I had known this before." Do you want to see a man grow into Christ-likeness? Teach him to fulfill his basic responsibility to his family. The families will love you for it!

Many people are involved in functional leadership groups. These would include deacon or trustee boards, finance groups, ushers, and committees. We lose an opportunity to create and enhance a discipling climate when we see these groups only in light of their functions. Does the chairman of the deacon board or of the finance committee see his responsibility as just conducting the necessary business of that group? Are prayer, fellowship, and discussion of Scripture among the activities of these groups? Do the chairmen of these groups feel a responsibility to encourage, stimulate, and show personal interest in the individuals in the groups? Can a finance chairman sense a spiritual ministry in conducting the committee business? Everything we do ought to contribute to discipleship, even business meetings. Do people come home from these kinds of groups feeling spiritually refreshed or feeling battered? An attitude of ministry ought to pervade our churches' functional groups. It is satisfying to see our deacons and their wives together for dinner or the ushers having a Saturday breakfast together. Fellowship and caring preoccupy us — and they should — if a thirst for Christ-likeness is to pervade our bodies.

Discipling and Church Growth

Discipleship enhances quantitative growth because of the attractiveness of the church's life. When people are growing and changing, nonmembers will be attracted.

Qualitative growth will be obvious. People will be eager to grow. A discipling climate will exist. Needs will be met. People will be cared for. They will be involved in the various levels of activity — the subcongregation and the cell.

Organically the church will grow because spiritual gifts will be an issue. As people minister, leadership positions will be filled. Leaders will be worked with on a personal basis. Training will take place. Functional ministry groups will operate smoothly because they will foster relationships, instead of dealing only with business details.

Action Items

List those involved in technical discipleship in your church. Are your leaders being discipled in this way?

What specific actions could you take to improve the corporate discipleship in your church?

Evaluate the discipling climate in your church.

feeding ministry	(poor) 1_____	10 (excellent)
discipling ministry	1_____	10
ministry to family	1_____	10
example of leaders	1_____	10

Suggest ways to improve the weakest area here.

Bibliography

Coleman, Robert E. *The Master Plan of Evangelism*. Old Tappan, NJ: Revell, 1978.

Hartman, Doug, and Sutherland, Doug. *Guidebook to Discipleship*. Irvine, CA: Harvest House, 1976.

Henrichsen, Walter A. *Disciples Are Made —Not Born*. Wheaton, IL: Victor Books, 1974.

Jenson, Ronald. "Gearing the Local Church for Discipleship." Doctoral dissertation, Western Conservative Baptist Seminary, 1975. Figure 3 and the information about discipling climate come from this dissertation.

World Wide Discipleship Association, Navigators, Churches Alive, and Campus Crusade for Christ. Each organization offers training programs.

14

Training

T raining and discipleship are related principles. Discipleship is the development of a person into Christ-likeness. Training is an integral part of discipling. Training is the process by which Christ-like behavior and character become a way of life through repeated, consistent application of God's truth. Training aims at developing the habitual right response. The twin principles of discipleship and training determine the church's qualitative development. Without implementing these principles, church growth cannot occur because without training and discipleship the church has no attracting power.

Definition of Training

Training is an activity which by its nature involves repetition. In I Timothy 4:7 (NASB) Paul tells Timothy, "discipline yourself for the purpose of godliness." The word *discipline* is used of an athlete practicing gymnastic exercises. Training involves practice. Practice involves repeating an exercise or technique until the skills developed become second nature and a way of life. Paul is telling Timothy to practice for godliness. The objective is for godliness to become a way of life. Hebrews 5:14 gives us the same idea: "But solid food is for the mature, who by constant use have trained themselves to distinguish good from evil." Discerning good and evil occurs through practice in the life of a mature disciple. He repeatedly makes the right choice when confronted with temptation, until the right response is second nature.

Parental training of children involves the same process. Wisdom, in the Book of Proverbs, means the discernment between right and wrong. Through discipline or training we are trying to cause our children to make the right choices when confronted with the choice between good and evil. The child is instructed by the parent. If the child disobeys or does not heed the instruction he is disciplined. The goal of the discipline is not to provide a vent for our displeasure; the goal is consistent right choices — wisdom — on the part of the child. Deuteronomy 6:5– 9 shows us the process. God's words are consistently taught and demonstrated by the parents in the home. The children apply the teaching, with discipline as an aid, until the teaching results in godly habits.

Jesus' training of the twelve disciples follows the same pattern. He repeatedly placed them in impossible situations in order to teach them to trust Him explicitly. Faith had to become second nature to them. It had to be a habitual response, because when He left to go back to the Father they would need to depend totally and completely on Him.

From these examples we would define training as teaching applied repeatedly in a person's life until the application becomes a habit.

The truths of the teaching transform the behavior and character of the disciple. Truths do so by repeated application to specific areas of life. Truth masters the person.

Training Contrasted with Teaching

There is a difference between teaching and training. You can teach without training and you can absorb teaching without being trained. You cannot, however, be trained without being taught. Teaching is a vital part of the training process but it can occur without resulting in training.

Teaching involves the impartation of knowledge, facts, or information. The truth of God as revealed uniquely in the Scripture is the starting point for developing wisdom. Teaching (the impartation of knowledge) isolated from training can be destructive and dangerous. I Corinthians 8:1 tells us that knowledge "puffs up" (NIV) or "makes arrogant" (NASB).

Training aims at the transformation of lifestyle. The goal of teaching is the application of the truth in such a way that behavior and character are being gradually changed into that of Jesus Christ. Training is not a one-time application of truth. It involves repeated application until godly habits are developed.

The problem with this whole process is that listening to teaching and amassing more information are easy. Training involves the discipline of getting the truth into one's life, and that is not easy. We are told that in order for anything to become a habit it has to be repeated at least forty times. For example, one of the authors began swimming regularly some time ago. The first time he watched others swimming laps he thought he could never match their endurance and strength. They would go up and down the length of the pool with no apparent effort. He did one lap and almost had a heart attack. It was discouraging and agonizing, but he persisted. Every time he swam he attempted to add one lap. After several weeks he was swimming much further with much less pain than when he started. What was the difference? It was repetition and practice.

The tragedy in our churches today is the lack of training. We love teaching. Teaching is necessary, but consistent, repetitive application of truth is equally necessary.

The transformation of life produced by training is a threefold process. The Book of Proverbs is a book about wisdom. This book presents wisdom to us as the product of knowledge and understanding (Prov. 2:6). Knowledge is the accumulation of information. Understanding is the application to our lives. Wisdom is the transformation of heart and character which results. The Spirit of God imparts to us deep insight into truth when that truth is conscientiously applied to life. Colossians 1:9 exhorts us to be filled "... with the knowledge of His will through all spiritual wisdom and understanding." The objective is in verse 10, "... that you may live a life worthy of the Lord. ..."

Factual information is never the goal. The goal is always truth, which results in a certain kind of walk. In I Thessalonians 2 Paul reviews his activity, which included grueling labor, among the believers in Thessalonica. He states the purpose for his effort in verse 12, "so that you may *walk* in a manner worthy of the God who calls you into His own kingdom and glory" (NASB, italics ours).

The training part of the process—the repetitive application of truth— is beautifully done in small groups. So much of our teaching tends to be academic. The small group allows people to study Scripture and then practice what they learn. Some churches have correct doctrinal statements and emphasize the teaching of the Word but experience division, apathy, and other problems. Rarely does such a church have a healthy small-group structure.

In the Christian Leadership Training Center for pastors, we have tried to always emphasize the practical implications of Scripture. Pastors are used to the opposite emphasis. We try to give specific projects to help them translate the knowledge into practice. The goal is the walk, the character, and the behavior. Hebrews 12:5–11 sums it up. Verse 11 says, "No discipline seems pleasant at the time, but painful. Later on, however, it produces a harvest of righteousness and peace for those who have been trained by it." The result of the repeated discipline of the Word is a certain kind of righteous character which can never be produced by teaching alone.

The Process of Training

We use the four training methods of Christ as the basis for a description of the training process. Those methods are instruction, demonstration, involvement, and evaluation.

Instruction

The first step Jesus used to bring truth into people's lives was instruction. Instruction involves three things.

First, Jesus' teaching was always done in the context of people's lives. His teaching was aimed at meeting needs. In Mark 3:14, we read that "He appointed twelve ... that they might be with Him and that He might send them out to preach...." The first priority was the personal association with His men. Jesus called these men into a full-time relationship to Himself. The method would not be the same today. We cannot spend all of our time in intimate relationships with church members. The principle is nonetheless valid. Do we teach in a context that applies to people's lives? Do our church people see the connection between what they hear on Sunday morning and specific situations that they face during the week? Even Jesus' words were practical. He used familiar terms, illustrations, and parables. He spoke of shepherds, vines, soils. He drew parallels between what he was teaching and familiar situations. He never taught doctrine for doctrine's sake.

He was never academic. His teaching always had a connection to people's lives. People always had to struggle with the implications of the teaching.

This is not to imply that the disciples understood perfectly the implications. Some of the implications were not fully understood until after Pentecost. The disciples had difficulty with their messianic expectations and their understanding of the kingdom and their role in it. Jesus' teaching about these subjects stimulated their questions, curiosity, and interest. He always stimulated them to ask, "But what does that mean?"

Second, the content of Jesus' instruction was always aimed at developing behavior and character traits in the disciples. They came into their relationship to Him with all kinds of prejudices and attitudes that needed to be changed. The Beatitudes are examples of His teaching. They are aimed at character development, not merely at imparting information. Paul echoes this objective when he tells Timothy in I Timothy 1:5, "But the goal of this command is love, which comes from a pure heart, a good conscience and a sincere faith." The goal was not an "A" on a written exam to show how well Timothy retained factual information, but the goal was development of a certain kind of character. In I Timothy 3 and Titus 1 Paul teaches about the qualifications for the office of elder. The qualities listed reflect a preoccupation with the kind of man — his character — rather than his capabilities. In II Peter 1:2– 10 Peter deals with the same issue. After listing numerous character qualities, he says that these qualities are the goal (v. 8), that if one does not aim at them as the goal he is blind or shortsighted (v. 9), and that the practice of them will guarantee that one will never stumble (v. 10). Paul again focuses on character in Galatians 5:22– 23. The "fruit of the Spirit" is described in terms of nine characteristics.

The emphasis on behavior change and character development is found throughout the New Testament in beautiful balance with the doctrinal sections. The arrangement of the various sections of Scripture emphasizes the fact that teaching is aimed at the development of a certain kind of person and walk.

Third, the instruction of Jesus was aimed much more at developing character than capabilities, but He did send the disciples out on occasion into situations where certain preaching skills could be developed. This emphasis on skill development is secondary at best.

Instruction in the church must have the same goal. We are interested in character development primarily, and character is developed through repeated practice and discipline. Ministry skills in the church need to be developed according to believers' gifts. For example, teachers need to be instructed about effective teaching methods. People need to be taught how to "do," but primarily how to "be."

Demonstration

Jesus not only instructed, but He also demonstrated the instruction. This was the reason for being "with them" (Mark 3:14). The disciples saw His character and skills. Our homes and churches are perfect places to display truth. All of us are imitators. Paul reminded the Thessalonians in I Thessalonians 1:6 that they had become "imitators of us and the Lord. . . ."

An example will clarify this point. The wife of one of the authors was rather upset with him when he ignored her pleas to be quiet in the morning when he awakened. Despite repeated requests, he did not understand. One day when he came home, she took him into the bedroom and told him to lie on the bed, close his eyes, and pretend he was asleep. She then proceeded to reenact his morning routine. She turned the light on, slammed the dresser drawers, started the razor and hair dryer while the bathroom door was open, gargled, stepped into the shower, and sang. He saw the point. The request was purely academic. He did not see the need. When she demonstrated the routine, she communicated the object lesson.

The principle of demonstration is a powerful one and one often overlooked in the church. In the church, character and skills need to be shown. How often do we ask people to do jobs but never give them an opportunity to see the job done by someone else as part of the learning process? On-the-job training is seldom done. Without it, the person asked to do the job is frustrated because he is not properly equipped. The whole body suffers because the quality of ministry is poor. Ideally no one would lead a ministry, teach a class, or preside at a committee meeting unless he or she had had an opportunity to observe a qualified person demonstrating the skills necessary to do the job. In this observation process, the necessary skills would not only be displayed, but the godly reponse to the pressure involved and other Christ-like character traits also would be demonstrated. In the average church the lack of emphasis on on-the-job training has produced a severe problem. Since proper training has not been done to date, it is difficult to train anyone else. Most churches need qualified people for the ministries. If we have untrained and unqualified people in positions of responsibility we do not want anyone else observing them. It becomes a vicious cycle. Ask yourself, "If I wanted to institute a Sunday-school teacher-in-training program, where would I put a potential teacher for three months so he or she could observe how it ought to be done?" If a name or names come to mind, new potential teachers should be sent to those classes on a rotating basis. The same would be true of the home Bible-study ministry. Potential home Bible-study leaders need to observe a successful study so that the potential leaders can see how it is done. The same is true in the other ministries. In every area of ministry, a model or models need to be developed so that others can come to see it in action.

Involvement

Jesus not only demonstrated character and skills, but He also involved His men in the process. They were continually looking over His shoulder, and were involved in His ministry. We learn by doing. We observe the model to get an idea of how a task ought to be done, but the real learning takes place when we do the work. Remember, training involves practice.

The way to involve people in specific church ministries is progressively. Again we will use the example of a Sunday-school teacher. To become a teacher in our Sunday school involves a process. That process begins with observation and moves through helping and occasional teaching until the person is ready to lead a class and take someone else through the same process. We never like to give anyone in any ministry the total responsibility right away. We like to do it in several stages. Most churches have such a leadership dilemma that it is not a matter of preparing people, but a matter of getting any person in the position. If gradual involvement of people in ministry is not an option now, it is an ideal that all of us need to begin to pray about and move toward. Begin to send people into Sunday-school classes, the nursery, and the usher corps as assistants. Let them see how the work is done. See if those people develop a deeper interest and commitment. If so, give them more significant responsibility. If this kind of process is not developed we will be putting people into leadership too quickly. A person needs to be developed for leadership. His or her faithfulness and teachability need to be tested. Observation and progressive involvement are necessary. Small jobs and then larger responsibilities are given as faithfulness is demonstrated.

Evaluation

Jesus exhibited character and skills, involved His men in the ministry, and He evaluated their progress. Evaluation allowed the disciples to go on to the next level of development. Jesus rebuked Peter when an obvious character flaw became apparent and said to him, "Get thee behind me, Satan." He was pointing out the source of Peter's thoughts and innovations. He was not afraid to rebuke and correct because this was an integral part of the training process.

Evaluation of lives and ministries in the church is sometimes difficult, as we have pointed out before. It is hard to evaluate volunteer labor, but essential. Evaluation of life and character begins with the application of the Word. We must not be judgmental. We can lovingly refer to the Word in specific situations and point out deviations from God's standards. Remember that the success of evaluation is the relationship with the person. That person must know that we love him and are committed to him.

In evaluating ministries and skills, we must emphasize agreed-on expectations and the expressed desire to help to develop a person into God's man and the leader God means him to be. Evaluation is not synonymous with criticism and judgment. Evaluation is encouragement, help, and commitment. Sometimes it becomes necessary to relieve a person of a leadership position. If this is the case, it is done lovingly but firmly. Usually this is necessary, we have found, when a person is in a position that does not correspond to his gift. He does not function because he is not doing what he should be doing in the body. We may relieve him of one position but need to help him discover where he can best serve within the body. Above all the person needs to sense and feel our commitment and support. This was certainly true of the disciples in their relationship to Jesus.

Training and Church Growth

The principle of training is central to church growth and health because it influences the qualitative development of the church. Character change occurs—and this is the purpose of the church. People are equipped and enabled to minister to others. This process will depend to some extent on the ability of the church to develop a staff. People are needed with the expertise to instruct and equip people in areas such as Christian education. A pastor cannot provide the time or expertise needed to develop people adequately in every area. Church leaders will need to pray about finding staff members who can provide equipping and training in specialized areas of ministry.

Quantitatively, training helps members to hone their ministry skills, and more ministries develop. More needs can be met. Thus, more people are attracted to the church.

Organic growth will be affected because leadership positions will be filled with qualified people. Ministries will develop qualitatively. People will be developed to gradually assume leadership in the areas of their spiritual gifts.

Action Items

The following questions will help determine the training available in your church and will indicate if that training meets present needs. Answer each question briefly and accurately.

> May the God of peace, . . . equip you with everything good for doing his will, and may he work in us what is pleasing to him, through Jesus Christ, to whom be glory for ever and ever. Amen. (Heb. 13:20–21)

1. What training does your church offer? Do you have a course listing with topic and enrollment?

2. What is the purpose of each training class?

3. How do the training classes fit with the overall purpose of your church? (Example: Evangelism Training—Our church is called to reach out to the lost)

4. Are the members of the church aware of how the training classes develop the purpose of your church?
   yes _____ no _____ unsure _____

5. What is the attitude toward the training offered?

6. How would you rate the training classes?
   a. The purpose of each class is clearly defined.
   always _____ occasionally _____ infrequently _____

b. Classes are meeting their stated purposes.
always _____ occasionally _____ infrequently _____

c. The training classes, in general, are growing.
yes _____ no _____ unsure _____

d. Are there classes which are declining?
yes _____ no _____
Which ones?
Why are they declining?
_____ not meeting needs
_____ not well taught
_____ difficulty of subject
_____ other_____

e. What would you like to see developed in the training classes?
_____ more variety
_____ more practical application (doing)
_____ more reference to the Bible
_____ more "how-tos" explained (discussing)
_____ more personal development
_____ other_____

7. Describe the training of children, youth, and adults.

a. Strength of ministries
Children 1.
            2.
            3.
Youth 1.
        2.
        3.
Adults 1.
         2.
         3.

b. Weaknesses of ministries
Children 1.
            2.
            3.
Youth 1.
        2.
        3.
Adults 1.
         2.
         3.

c. What percent of resources is expended?

$$
\begin{array}{rl}
\text{Budget—Children} & \rule{2cm}{0.4pt} \\
\text{Youth} & \rule{2cm}{0.4pt} \\
\text{Adults} & \rule{2cm}{0.4pt} \\
& \text{100 percent}
\end{array}
$$

$$
\begin{array}{rl}
\text{Church Structure—Children} & \rule{2cm}{0.4pt} \\
\text{Youth} & \rule{2cm}{0.4pt} \\
\text{Adults} & \rule{2cm}{0.4pt} \\
\text{For all} & \rule{2cm}{0.4pt} \\
& \text{100 percent}
\end{array}
$$

Time—Within Church Body   Outside Church Body

	Within Church Body	Outside Church Body
Children	_____	_____
Youth	_____	_____
Adults	_____	_____

Subtotal + Subtotal = 100 percent

8. Please make any additional comments you believe would improve the quality of the training classes.

9. Identify the committee responsible for overseeing all training.

10. Describe the organizational makeup of this committee (subcommittees, consultants, participative leadership). Is it representative of the church in age and interest?

11. What responsibilities is the training committee expected to fulfill?

12. What percentage of the church membership is training to minister to the body of Christ and to minister to nonbelievers?
Body of Christ _____ Nonbelievers _____

13. What training materials are used in your church?

14. How are the materials chosen? Has your church studied cost as it relates to the degree of effectiveness of the materials?

Evaluate how specific ministries within your church rate according to the training principles listed in this chapter. A rating of "1" means the ministry is weak; a rating of "5" means the program is strong.

Training Principle

1. _____

Instruction	1 2 3 4 5
Context	1 2 3 4 5
Content	1 2 3 4 5
Character	1 2 3 4 5
Capabilities	1 2 3 4 5
Demonstration	1 2 3 4 5
Involvement	1 2 3 4 5
Evaluation	1 2 3 4 5

2. _____

Instruction	1 2 3 4 5
Context	1 2 3 4 5
Content	1 2 3 4 5
Character	1 2 3 4 5
Capabilities	1 2 3 4 5
Demonstration	1 2 3 4 5
Involvement	1 2 3 4 5
Evaluation	1 2 3 4 5

3. _____

Instruction	1 2 3 4 5
Context	1 2 3 4 5
Content	1 2 3 4 5
Character	1 2 3 4 5
Capabilities	1 2 3 4 5
Demonstration	1 2 3 4 5
Involvement	1 2 3 4 5
Evaluation	1 2 3 4 5

Bibliography

Coleman, Robert E. *The Master Plan of Evangelism*. Old Tappan, NJ: Revell, 1978.

Hartman, Doug, and Sutherland, Doug. *Guidebook to Discipleship*. Irvine, CA: Harvest House, 1976.

Henrichsen, Walter A. *Disciples Are Made—Not Born*. Wheaton, IL: Victor Books, 1974.

International Conference for Learning. Gospel Light teacher-training program.

Jenson, Ronald. "Gearing the Local Church for Discipleship." Doctoral dissertation, Western Conservative Baptist Seminary, 1975. This includes information about the four training principles.

Richards, Lawrence O. *Creative Bible Teaching*. Chicago: Moody, 1970.

World Wide Discipleship Association, Navigators, Churches Alive, and Campus Crusade for Christ. Each organization offers training programs.

15

Evangelism

Evangelism is central to any discussion of church growth or health. It is one of those foundational principles on which everything else rests. The church will not, indeed cannot, grow unless it evidences a corporate concern for extending its message to the world. The emphasis in the Book of Acts is on the influence of the church in ever-widening circles until the whole world would feel the impact (Acts 1:8). In I Thessalonians 1:7–8 Paul expresses wonder and joy as he tells the church at Thessalonica that its faith has sounded forth and has had a lasting impact on people far beyond its locale. Such is the biblical pattern. The extension of the gospel to the world beyond the walls of the church is the mission of the church.

If we are to understand this principle, we need to understand several things about the nature of evangelism. Many pastors and church leaders today are troubled by the tension they feel within themselves and their people during any discussion about evangelism. Some have tried to adopt parachurch form, methodology, and training, with little lasting success. Parachurch methodology for the most part has been developed in a nonbody context. The emphasis is on the intense, structured, one-to-one approach which is the natural emphasis when evangelism is not being done in a church context. It is usually outstanding training for communicating the gospel's basic content, but it is not geared for assimilating new believers into the church. Therefore, the church needs to find ways to enhance this training. We need desperately a philosophy

179

of evangelism which takes into account, in the development of specific methodology, the functions of a healthy church.

We will consider first the nature of evangelism and then explain the development of a methodology which can be carried out in a growing, healthy body of believers.

The Nature of Evangelism

The nature of evangelism will bear on the development of a biblical philosophy.

A Three-Part Process

Part of the problem in developing a consistent philosophy of evangelism is our tendency to make evangelism—as we define it—an end in itself. God never intended that. We consider evangelism primarily a human effort to get a certain collection of theological facts before people and to do it in such a way that the presentation culminates in a "decision" based on those facts. This activity is generally seen as an effort made in and of itself with little awareness of how it fits into the working of God's Spirit in the person's life. This effort of extending a certain message (evangelism) to another person or group of people is important. But evangelism has to be seen as a much larger process by which God moves into a life. This process involves three stages, all of them superintended by God's Spirit, although He will use human instrumentality to accomplish them. The first is a preconversion process known as *conviction* (John 16:7– 11). The second is *conversion* itself or the point of transfer from the "kingdom of darkness" to the "kingdom of His beloved son" (Col. 1:13). The third step is a postconversion process of *growth and maturation* (I Peter 2:2).

Conviction

The first stage in God's total work in a life is conviction. This is an overlooked step in the discussion of evangelism. This word describes God's approach to the darkened, hardened heart of the sinner (Eph. 2:1). Conviction is preparatory. It describes the way God begins to awaken a desire and create a thirst in the heart. It is that sense that a need exists, that an emptiness and vacuum is there. John 16:7– 11 is the classic passage which describes this work of the Spirit. It tells us that the conviction concerns sin, righteousness, and judgment. God's Spirit begins to move in such a way in the heart that a person begins to wrestle with these three issues and their implications.

Conversion is a pivotal stage in the total process but still only one part. It is the entry point into God's family, but much precedes that entry and much follows it. Jesus' use of the term "born again" (John 3:3) to describe conversion was not a chance choice of words. It beautifully describes conversion's place in the total process. Natural birth is preceded by a process of preparation and is followed by a lifetime of growth and maturation. The new birth is preceded by the process of conviction and preparation and is followed by the sanctification process, also a continuous work of the Holy Spirit.

James Engel, in *What's Gone Wrong with the Harvest?*, has developed what has come to be known as the Engel scale (Figure 4). It is a description, by way of a numerical scale, of this whole process, especially the preconversion stage. It makes clear the issue of a progression toward a decision. It illustrates how God moves a person toward conversion, and the various issues at each point. This preconversion stage is no less supernatural than the actual conversion point. God is working in ways unique to the individual. He is using various means and a personal, individualized timetable to move each person through the process toward an honest, genuine "new birth." The process cannot be rushed, aborted, or manipulated by human effort.

When we are insensitive to where a person is in the conviction stage, we are likely to press for a decision before a person is able to make an honest one. When this happens, a "decision" may be registered but new birth may not occur. This is a major frustration with so many evangelism training programs. People are taught to go out, engage a person in minimal conversation, go through a gospel presentation, and invite the person to say a prayer. Many people will say a prayer. The evangelist is overjoyed and comes back to report these prayers and to register the decisions. Frustration sets in when an attempt is made to follow up the decisions. The evangelist discovers some people may be unwilling to meet with him, and often sees no signs of new life. After several such experiences, he becomes frustrated and concludes either that evangelism does not work or that the problem is poor follow-up technique or "bad soil." The problem generally is not the follow-up technique. It goes back further. The evangelist was trying to follow up a person who had not been adequately prepared to be born again. The evangelist may have invited him to make a decision he was not ready to make. A prayer had been said, but communication had not taken

Figure 4
Engel's Evangelistic "Countdown"*

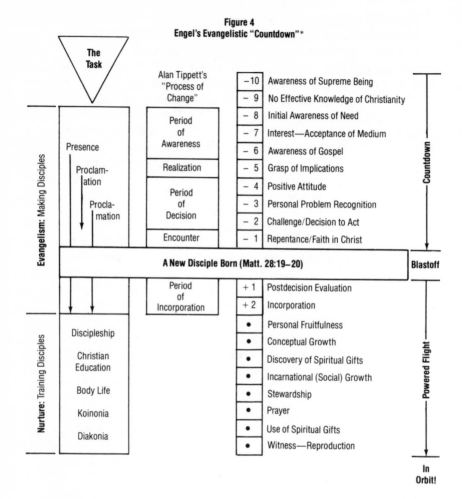

*Adapted from Figure 3, p. 45, of *What's Gone Wrong with the Harvest?* by James F. Engel and H. Wilbert Norton, copyright © 1975 by The Zondervan Corporation. Used by permission.

This model as presented here has undergone an interesting history. In rudimentary forms, it was first suggested by Viggo Sogaard while he was a student in the Wheaton Graduate School. It was later revised by James F. Engel and published in such sources as *Church Growth Bulletin* and elsewhere during 1973. Since that time, modifications have been introduced as others have made suggestions. Particularly helpful comments have been advanced by Richard Senzig of the communications faculty at the Wheaton Graduate School and Professors C. Peter Wagner and Charles Kraft of the Fuller School of World Mission.

"Process of Change" is from p. 123 of *Verdict Theology in Missionary Theory*, by Alan Tippett, published 1975. Used by permission of William Carey Library Publishers, PO Box 128-C, Pasadena, CA 91104, USA.

place. The process was rushed. If God is working in a life to convict a person and the process is discernibly underway, the time of the actual decision or transfer is not the issue.

We do not mean to imply that it is wrong to share the gospel with a stranger on an airplane, for example, or to aggressively invite the person to receive Christ as his Savior. We do not know precisely where people are in the conviction process. God may well use just a few minutes with a person in His conviction process. The encounter may stimulate thought, stir desires, and create a thirst for further investigation of Christ's claim. We must not hesitate to speak with anyone anywhere. What we must avoid is an undue focus on the decision.
undue focus on the decision.

In the conviction process, as the Holy Spirit moves a person toward conversion, three basic barriers must be overcome. These barriers must be neutralized before any genuine commitment can take place. The person being witnessed to will receive everything he hears through this three-part grid.

The first barrier is background. As you discuss the gospel facts with a person, he is sifting it through the grid of his past experiences with "religion," which were probably negative. The Holy Spirit must make the person understand the difference between religion and the gospel message. As long as he is equating what you are saying with his past religious experience, the chances are it will not make much sense. Religion has negative connotations to most people. Part of the convicting work of the Spirit is a sense that the gospel is "different." Many times people, after trusting Christ as Savior, have commented that as they heard the gospel, they sensed that they had heard all this before but for some reason it now made sense. People equate the message with many things in their background—primarily the religious symbols, rituals, and ceremonies of their childhood. These misconceptions and stereotypes need to be dealt with. The gospel must be clearly perceived as significant and having life-altering ramifications. We have prayed with many people to receive Christ who we believe may not have understood the gospel or its ramifications, although it was clearly and carefully explained. This is not to say that all of the theological ramifications of the gospel must be understood before a person can come to faith in Christ. It is to say that because of the work of the Spirit a person must see that the gospel message and the necessary response to it are not synonymous with the religious ceremony and ritual.

The second barrier to effective communication is the absence of perceived needs. The pattern of Jesus' ministry was to minister to people in the context of their needs. People are more receptive to hearing the gospel message when they see that it has relevance to their lives. Response to the gospel takes place when there is a sense of need. The Holy Spirit is able to use adverse situations—financial difficulty, death, or family crisis—to create a thirst in the heart or an awareness of need. Simply reciting the facts of the gospel to people will not trigger a sense that this message has relevance for and implications in their lives.

Sometimes we mistake a person's lack of overt antagonism to the gospel as openness and conviction. It may not be openness at all. It may simply be a tacit agreement with the facts. Many people have no intellectual disagreement with the facts—they have heard them all their lives. They are willing to acknowledge those facts. But the message has no relevance because they do not see how it affects anything today. They are not faced with a situation which would cause their real need (salvation) to surface as a perceived need. This is a work of the Holy Spirit. He alone can cause a person to sense the vacuum that exists within, to feel the emptiness. He alone can cause a person to make the connection between his perceived needs and the gospel message in terms of its ability to meet those needs. So many people have filled the void with material possessions, occupations, or sex. These things have dulled the senses and it takes the supernatural work of God's Spirit to awaken a person to his need, to create a thirst, and to draw him to Christ as the perceived answer to his need.

The third barrier to genuine communication is definitions. The great gospel words such as grace, sin, or blood have certain meanings to the evangelist. He cannot assume that the person being witnessed to is assigning the same definitions to the words and the same meaning to the concepts. That person may be interpreting the words in light of his background or other things. We have talked about the gospel with an individual, have seen him nod his head in agreement throughout the presentation, and even express a willingness to say a prayer of invitation to ask Christ into his life—only to reveal on questioning that his definition of terms was different.

The process of conviction by the Holy Spirit will deal with all three of these barriers. He will bring the person to an awareness that the gospel is not necessarily synonymous with his religious background. He will move a person to a sense of need and thirst and He will cause a person to understand the terms of the gospel. This whole preparation may occur quickly or involve a longer period of time. Whatever the length of time, and it will vary from person to person, the process will remove the barriers. There will be a deepening awareness of need. Understanding will blossom into desire. The decision or prayer is the simple expression of a desire that has been developing and a need that has been increasingly felt.

Our attempts to evangelize need to be characterized by sensitivity. To ignore the preparation stage is to encourage a premature birth. In seeking to be sensitive to a person's need, we must be aware of the three ingredients of believing faith. In John 20 we have examples of three kinds of needs, the meeting of which resulted in faith in Christ. The setting is the resurrection of Christ. Verse 8 tells us how John came to faith. It was through the meeting of an intellectual need.

> Finally the other disciple, who had reached the tomb first, also went inside. He *saw* and believed. (italics ours)

The word *saw* indicates more than physical sight. John "saw" the implications involved in what his eyes were seeing. His was a rational belief based on evidence. Many people come to Christ in the same way. Logically and rationally the gospel makes sense. The logical presentation of evidence is what triggers in many people the desire to follow Christ.

Verses 11–18 tell us how Mary came to believe that Christ was alive. She came primarily with an emotional need. To her it was a matter of the heart. She was not impressed with the evidence so much as a great sense of emptiness and hunger. It was in her case an attraction of the heart.

In verses 24–28 Thomas responds to Christ through the meeting of yet another need. To him belief was primarily a volitional issue. He had to have it his way. In verse 25 he says:

> Unless I see the nail marks in his hands and put my finger where the nails were, and put my hand into His side, *I will not believe it*. (italics ours)

In verse 27 we read that Jesus obliges him, meets him exactly where he is in the process, and invites him to put his hand on the wound. To Thomas it was a matter of will.

The intellect, emotion, and will were issues to some degree with these three, but each person had a predominant need that had to be met before faith would occur.

In the conviction process some will need an apologetic approach — the rational presentation of evidences. Not everyone will respond in this way. Some people will simply need to see the difference in the life of a friend or the love of a group to have the heart moved. Some will have a much better grasp of the theological issues inherent in the gospel. For others that understanding will come later. For some it is a matter of yielding the will. Whatever the need or the approach, God graciously and lovingly meets us just where we are and firmly moves us to genuine response.

We desperately need to learn to sensitively listen to people. Evangelism to many of us means telling someone something. More often than not it should involve a creative, discerning listening process. To prayerfully ask questions and listen to a person will provide clues as to the needs, the questions, the barriers, and the position of the person in the preparation process. Not everyone needs a gospel presentation right now. Not everyone needs to be confronted with the need for a decision right now. God will bring each one to those points in His time and we should know how to do both and be willing to do both if the person is at that point. The most important question to ask is, "Where is this person?" However, he may need to be urged toward making a decision.

Conversion

At the conclusion of conviction — and only God knows where that point is — conversion occurs. Conversion is the fruit of conviction. It is the point of the transfer referred to in Colossians 1:13. God's Spirit has been at work deep in the soul, doing His work of awakening, preparing, and drawing. He has used people, material, meetings, mass media, or other tools in His ministry. The person has moved from apathy or antagonism to a point of intense desire to know Christ. The process has been as miraculous as the process of conception and natural birth. Jesus is the only way to God (John 14:6), but there are many ways to approach Jesus. What a privilege to be used by the Spirit as part of the process to get a person ready to move from one sphere of spiritual experience (death) to another (life).

The actual point of decision and commitment, usually expressed in a prayer to receive Christ, is really anticlimactic. Belief occurs in the heart (Rom. 10:9–10). Conversion, like the marriage ceremony, is exciting and meaningful, but the commitment to one another was made long before. Conversion does not necessarily take place when a person reads or says a prayer. This may confirm a previous decision.

Maturation

The third stage of the larger process is growth or maturation. This is the postconversion process. Natural birth issues spontaneously in growth. Usually you do not have to work to make a baby grow. Feeding and care are essential but the growth is an inherent part of the process. Inadequate follow-up is not the only reason for nongrowth. Nonbirth is also a reason for nongrowth. Problems experienced in follow-up may be traced to the witnessing procedure. A decision may have been urged prematurely.

The church (the body of Christ) is God's primary methodology and provision for the growth process. If the church is healthy and functioning as God intended, conviction and conversion will be the natural result of the body's attractive qualities and maturation will occur as the natural result of its internal vigor.

Often in the parachurch organizations the process is segmented. The reason is that there is not the same internal energy to provide the natural climate for attraction and growth. Since the forms of ministry effective in the parachurch movements have been transferred into the church, the church has adopted a segmented approach to evangelism and for the most part does not see the process as a whole one. We have our people going door-to-door sharing the gospel to strangers who are inadequately prepared and then feeling frustrated and guilty when the decisions do not respond as we wish to our follow-up. This type of approach is good for training people in the mechanics of evangelism, but is one of the least effective ways for assimilating new converts into the church.

If the witnessing is sensitively done, and the birth is genuine and occurs in the body, then growth will occur because the life is genuine. Feeding and care are vital. The church has been designed by God to provide these services for the new spiritual babies. The church is designed to provide the full range of "one another" ministries that a new Christian needs to develop properly into maturity and Christ-likeness.

This brings up an important question. If a major goal is incorporation into a healthy body, what happens when someone who makes a decision either resists coming to church or is already part of a church where solid teaching and ministry are not available? Not every person we witness to will accompany us to our church the following Sunday.

A continued resistance to any kind of group follow-up activity may be a sign that the decision was not genuine. Real decisions result in a desire and eagerness to grow. An invitation to a Bible study or other group activities generally will not be resisted.

An invitation to church may be resisted because a person is already a part of another church. In this case a side-door approach to the church is needed. This approach involves a network of group activities which may or may not be sponsored by your church. These would include men's, women's, or couples' Bible studies which meet on neutral territory such as homes or offices.

Resisting invitations is a problem in areas where many people, even non-Christians, attend church regularly. When churched non-Christians make honest commitments to Christ they need to be put into contact with other believers who will help them to grow and who will encourage them. If good Bible teaching and growth opportunites are not available in their churches, then other group opportunites (e.g., home Bible-study groups) need to be available for them. We will say more about these opportunites when we discuss methodology.

Audio-Visual Process

The first point about the nature of evangelism was that evangelism is a unified process which includes a preconversion stage (conviction), a crisis point (conversion), and a postconversion stage (maturation).

The second major point about the nature of evangelism is that this process is an audio-visual one.

In reading the New Testament we have the impression that evangelism was a spontaneous by-product of natural processes within the church. People were attracted because something in the body was so attractive. People saw what took place in the corporate life of the church, and saw how the believers responded to the external pressure which constantly faced the church. We suspect that an organized, structured evangelism "program" with a full-time specialist would have been out of place.

Evangelism in the New Testament was not so much "done" as it was "occurring." Evangelism seems to have happened naturally. This is what Jesus seems to be saying to us in John 13:34– 35. There would be a genuineness about the relationships between the disciples which would be magnetic. Evangelism would spring from *koinonia*. There would be a magnetism about a body of people who love each other.

There is something powerful and effective about people who are trying to apply the facts or content of the gospel to their relationships with other people. It not only needs to be heard (audio), but also to be seen (visual). When you begin to hear comments such as, "I've never seen people like this before," or "I've never sensed love like this anywhere else," you will know that evangelism is taking place the way it was meant to.

In the church today we have lost the naturalness and spontaneity of the process. Evangelism is a struggle. It is programmed. It is structured. People feel guilty for not evangelizing. A call for people to come out for visitation turns out a mere handful. People are afraid to "witness." They fear hostile response or difficult questions. There is nothing natural about witnessing but people think that it should be.

Two bridges must be crossed which lead to incorporation into the body of Christ. One bridge is theological. This corresponds to the Engel scale. Factual issues relating to background, misconceptions, or definitions need to be resolved. The other bridge is sociological. This has to do with relationships or the context in which the whole process is happening. If people are being exposed to the content (hearing) without the relationships (seeing), the whole process will be short-circuited. Evangelism is not primarily an academic exercise.

God designed the church to attract people outside its fellowship through an audio-visual process. This is God's way of simultaneously crossing the theological and sociological bridges. If a church is to be a magnet, continually attracting people to its life, it must be healthy. The attraction is the climate of love, caring, and acceptance. If this climate does not exist, neither will the attraction. Many churches do not see the connection between a healthy body and evangelism. An unhealthy church will not be attractive. Sickness rarely attracts. We hear the statement sometimes that the church exists for the edification of the believer. This is true to a point. However, this philosophy tends to blur the fact that what happens "in here" has a marvelous power to attract those "out there." When Christians genuinely are excited about what is happening in and through their church it will be hard to keep non-Christians away. Non-Christians will appear in the most unlikely places.

Sometimes we are asked about the evangelism "program" in our church. We do some things primarily to share the gospel with outsiders, but everything we do attracts non-Christians. Non-Christians attend Sunday-school classes, home Bible studies, socials, seminars, and other activities. Why? Because Christians are excited about what God is doing. They are not embarrassed to bring a neighbor or a friend to any activity. Although the activity is intended for the Christian primarily, non-Christians are attracted.

Usually, if a church is not demonstrating this climate, any evangelism program for which you try to enlist people will fail. It is impossible to attract a non-Christian to something about which the Christians are not excited. One church we know continued to promote an evangelism program when it was experiencing problems. There were several competing factions, recriminations were common, and bitterness was rampant. If the goal of evangelism is incorporation into a body, this church had the cart before the horse.

We have discussed evangelism as an audio-visual, life-related process which includes conviction, conversion, and incorporation into a healthy body for growth, development, and maturation. We turn now to evangelism methodology in the church.

Methodology for Evangelism

How do we present the gospel of Christ to people? For every church the answer will be different because every church exists in its own cultural environment. What works for one will not work for another. We would like to suggest several ideas which we feel will help to stimulate thinking and experimentation. We must always keep the goal in mind. It is not *just* "decisions" or the numbers who have "accepted Christ." It is also the incorporation of people into the life of a body. And, ultimately, it is mature disciples (committed, reproducing believers). Conversion is a part of the whole process. In developing an evangelism methodology in the church, we must keep in mind the need to communicate the message of Christ as it affects lives.

Outreach Events

One effective way to witness is the evangelism "event." Events include men's breakfasts, women's luncheons, or dinners with a speaker and music. The purpose of these events is outreach. These events give Christians the opportunity to bring a neighbor, friend, or fellow worker to an interesting program in which the gospel will be presented in a low-key, yet clear, way.

Every two or three months, we sponsor a men's breakfast on a Saturday morning. We meet at a local hotel for a complete breakfast for which no charge is made. Donations are accepted at the conclusion. The program will usually consist of some introductory remarks by a master of ceremonies, a brief testimony by one of our men, and a speaker. Our speakers have included professional athletes, politicians, businessmen, and others who are able to explain how they came to know Christ personally. The meeting is closed in prayer and an opportunity to receive Christ is given. Comment cards are filled out and left on the tables.

A similar format characterizes a women's luncheon. This event may include music or a fashion show. We sponsor these luncheons two or three times a year as part of our women's ministry. The church also organizes similar events in all of our ministries, including singles, high school, and others.

Several principles need to be kept in mind in planning an outreach event.

First, the purpose is outreach. Every Christian needs to invite non-Christians to come with him or her. The program is aimed at the non-Christian. The message is a testimony. The emphasis is on the relevancy of a relationship with Christ. The purpose is not to give a full, complete explanation of the gospel; it is basic exposure to the message and to Christians. The event will not have succeeded if non-Christians are not there in substantial numbers. We like to see at least an equal ratio of Christians and non-Christians.

Next, the atmosphere is low-key. We want people to relax and enjoy the event. At our breakfasts, it is beautiful to watch the guests talking to other men about sports, politics, and business. Many non-Christian men have never met other men who are interested in the same things they are interested in and who also have a relationship with Christ. The speakers talk about the gospel but in a way that the non-Christians can identify with.

Finally, any church can hold these events. You do not have to start with a huge event. A church can use two or three of its own men or women to give testimonies about how they came to Christ. Our first men's breakfast was attended by only twenty men. A pastor could give a simple talk about "the relevancy of Christ in a man's world" or something similar. An event does not have to be elaborate or expensive. Success depends on the atmosphere and the presence of non-Christians.

Outreach events offer several benefits.

One benefit is that a person is exposed to the message in a group setting. The goal of evangelism is to fold the new convert into a fellowship where he or she can grow into maturity. This goal is more easily realized when the gospel is presented to a group.

Another benefit is that it is easy to invite a non-Christian. A non-Christian will be more likely to accept an invitation to a Saturday morning breakfast than a Sunday morning worship service. Part of the problem that churches have with evangelism is that it seems to frightening. Say "evangelism" to the average church member and the word will conjure up images of door-to-door witnessing, trying to answer impossible-to-answer questions, or doors slammed in his face. An event simplifies the process. The event does not "seem" to be evangelism.

A final benefit is that an event is easy to follow up. It is easy, on the way home, to ask the guest what he thought of the event, if the speaker made sense to him or her, and other questions which will help to discern the person's spiritual situation. It may be possible to lead the person to Christ at that time. An event almost always allows an opportunity for further discussion. It is easy to offer personal testimony. The one-to-one contact is much more open after an event because the program gives the basis for further conversation about its content in a natural, spontaneous way.

It has been our experience that non-Christians are rarely negative about what they hear. The comment cards usually reveal positive response. The reason is that the atmosphere is low-key, pressure-free, and enjoyable.

Need-Oriented Seminars

A second way to draw non-Christians close to the body of Christ is through seminars which relate to specific needs that Christians and non-Christians have in common. These seminars, unlike outreach events, are not directed specifically at the non-Christian, but the non-Christian will attend because of the subject matter. We have held seminars which have included topics such as time management (men, women, or couples); parenting (men, women, or couples); leadership in the home (men); maximum marriage (couples); career development (singles and/or couples); women's physical problems (taught by a Christian gynecologist and his wife); financial planning; or dating when single (never married, divorced, separated, or widowed). Many times we have conducted these seminars for our own people and have not developed them as outreach programs, but always there are non-Christians who attend because the topics deal with needs.

programs, but always there are non-Christians who attend because the topics deal with needs.

These seminars can be scheduled for two or three successive Saturday mornings, two or three mornings or afternoons, all day Saturday, or several evenings. It is best not to make them long-running programs.

A church can be creative in its choice of topics. Take advantage of the expertise in the congregation. We heard of one church that used a mechanic to teach neighborhood men to do minor tune-ups and auto repairs. The principle is to find out what people need and attempt to meet the need. There are needs which are common to everyone, whether Christian or non-Christian.

These seminars are not explicitly evangelistic. The gospel is included if it can be done naturally. The main advantage is the contact with non-Christians in a nonthreatening way. These programs are beautifully used by the Lord to open doors for further ministry in people's lives.

Other Outreach Possibilities

Other possibilities for outreach are exciting and creative. We will list them so you can think about them.

1. Children's activities, such as weekly boys' and girls' clubs and camps
2. Recreational activities—gym nights, swim parties, or ball games
3. Social activities, such as potluck dinners or class parties
4. Home Bible studies
5. Home entertaining—dinner parties with non-Christians invited—which may include a speaker and program
6. Neighborhood coffees with speaker and testimonies

All of these—and other—potential outreach activities are used to expose the non-Christians to the message of Christ in a group setting. These activites provide opportunity to do outreach in a natural and positive way. Follow-up is natural. Such programs are truly audio-visual in nature. Every church will do different things. An inner-city church may have a block party. A suburban church might sponsor a men's breakfast program in a beautiful hotel. The point is that we must make it easy and natural for Christians to reach out to their neighbors and friends. Evangelism has been too narrowly defined. We have limited it to "going out to tell them," which implies a door-to-door methodology which is unexciting and unrelated to life. People out there are hurting. Marriages are collapsing and parenting is a frightening experience. All kinds of social and spiritual needs are there to be met. A church has been planted in a community to meet those needs. Any methodology which does not include ways to meet needs, and in the process draw people close to the body of Christ, is inadequate. The church is in a beautiful position to minister to people because it has a power and magnetism that does not exist in any other organization in the world.

Training for Evangelism

The outreach training needs of a church will be largely determined by outreach methodology. Training is needed. The questions are, "how much?" and "what kind?"

We believe that every believer needs to know how to bring another person to a point of decision and commitment to Christ. Some basic training is needed. We need to follow up contacts with visitors and new residents in the community. For these contacts and ministries, training and procedures are needed.

Training needs to correspond to methodology. If the methodology calls for simple door-to-door saturation efforts, then intense training will be needed for this one-on-one approach. If the methodology calls for an event, then the training will need to correspond to that approach.

We would suggest that a training program such as Evangelism Explosion or Campus Crusade for Christ be implemented and that as many people as possible learn how to lead another individual to Christ. At the same time we would urge that training be available which relates to the interpersonal aspects of the process—outreach events, home entertaining, or follow-up of group outreach functions.

The problem with most evangelism training given in the church is that the training is imported from the parachurch organizations and focuses on the need for a decision, overlooks the totality of the process, and does not take advantage of the natural attracting power of a healthy body. Since training does not focus on what is natural, it is difficult to maintain any momentum.

Any training process must maintain the balance between the technical, one-on-one explanation of the gospel and the corporate aspects of the process. Both are needed and both are needed in balance.

The point is that evangelism is vital to a healthy church. People are lost without Christ, and we *must* aggressively, tactfully, sensitively, and deliberately communicate the love of God and forgiveness in Christ to them. This should be done in a way that will see them assimilated into our healthy churches.

Action Items

List the types of evangelistic activities in your church.

List names of those who have been effectively evangelized and absorbed into your church this past year.

What need in your community "target audience" could be met through a creative evangelistic event? Suggest when and how this event could take place.

Bibliography

Body Evangelism. Pasadena, CA: Charles E. Fuller Institute of Evangelism and Church Growth, n.d.

Bright, Bill. *How to Be Sure You're a Christian.* Arrowhead Springs, CA: Campus Crusade for Christ, n.d.

_____. *How to Experience God's Love and Forgiveness.* Arrowhead Springs, CA: Campus Crusade for Christ, n.d.

Engel, James F., and Norton, H. Wilbert. *What's Gone Wrong with the Harvest?* Grand Rapids: Zondervan, 1975.

Evangelism Explosion used by the Coral Ridge Presbyterian Church. Based on information from Campus Crusade for Christ and the Fuller Evangelistic Association.

Falwell, Jerry. *Capturing a Town for Christ.* Old Tappan, NJ: Revell, 1973.

Griffin, Em. *The Mind Changers.* Wheaton, IL: Tyndale, 1976.

Wagner, C. Peter. *Your Church Can Grow.* Glendale, CA: Regal, 1976.

Summary

We have discussed fifteen principles involved in building a healthy church. A healthy church will grow. We cannot make it grow. It will grow because it is a living organism and living organisms grow if they remain healthy.

Careful diagnosis should tell us the state of our church's health. After studying the principles from Scripture we should be able to isolate areas that need work. If this book has done nothing else than help in this diagnostic process, it has accomplished something significant. In summary, several things need to be kept in mind.

The treatment of these principles was not meant to be exhaustive. We have merely tried to isolate principles. The forms, methods, and specific procedures of implementation will vary among individual churches. Every church exists in its own cultural environment, has its unique problems and opportunities, and will implement the principles of Scripture in different ways. The principles, however, will be true in every situation. They are cross-cultural. It is important to work from principle to method and form. Usually we reverse this order. We have intended to stimulate thinking about principles. Much work needs to be done in each of the areas covered. Philosophy and principles about church growth are given to us in the Scripture, particularly the Epistles; these concepts need to be further defined and applied.

It is important to grasp the relationship of the principles. At first glance the principles seem totally unrelated. We will miss the impact if we see them that way. It is difficult to isolate the principles because they are so interrelated and interdependent. Several of the principles are like threads which run through the whole process of developing health. These principles include prayer, purpose, climate, and diagnosis. These principles apply in every principal area. Without all of them operating, the individual principles cannot be fully effective and full health cannot be attained. Leadership, for example, is developed in prayer, in a climate of involvement, during and after diagnosis, and always with a sense of the church's purpose. The same is true of planning, small groups, or any of the others.

Several principles relate specifically to the internal structure of the church. These would include, but not be limited to, celebration (worship), small groups, subcongregations (absorption), lay involvement, leadership, training, and discipleship. All of these principles relate to each other. Small groups are linked to subcongregations and leadership is a principle common to both of them. Discipleship is the purpose for the internal structure. Training is a principle common to every internal program. To the extent that any of these are not being implemented, to that extent the church will not reach its full discipling and evangelizing potential.

Several of the principles relate specifically to the management process for both the whole church and the individual ministries. These principles include diagnosis, planning, priorities, and programming, with purpose as the thread running through all of them. In each church ministry (e.g., Sunday school or youth), this process will be fully implemented as well as in the overall ministry. The pastor and the governing body will spearhead the process in the church and the people in charge of individual ministries will do that in their respective areas. In the large church, full-time staff will more than likely develop the process in their areas of specialization. The process will include program design, budgeting, scheduling, and control. Remember that we defined management in the broad sense. It does not mean merely administration, but the process of overseeing the movement of a body toward its objectives and the fulfillment of its purpose.

The implementation of the principles will take time. We cannot be discouraged if every principle is not being fully applied at this moment. Every church, no matter how far along in the process, will have progress to make in some of the areas. Some initial steps will enable a pastor and his church to start implementing principles.

Diagnose the overall ministry and the individual ministries. Isolate needs, determine the state of leadership, evaluate budget, facility, and staff. Work from facts, not from supposition. Take surveys and do other fact-gathering exercises.

Write a clear purpose statement. Involve the governing body and others in its formulation. Preach about it. Communicate it in writing and through other means.

Determine what needs to be and can be done to strengthen and/or change the church constitution and by-laws to provide more flexibility in the selection of leaders.

Develop—through preaching, teaching, example, and structure—an emphasis on prayer. This is a key to everything, including climate. If this is not being done, every other effort will be to no avail.

Start to work on specific job descriptions, beginning with the pastor and governing body and working down to ministry heads and those who report to them. In addition, work on a churchwide organizational chart which will give an overview of the present leadership situation and the relationship of people within the leadership structure.

The objective is people, not machinery. Everything we have talked about is geared toward the development of a certain kind of person. We are being used by the Lord to move people toward Christ-likeness. This is the great calling of the pastoral ministry. The organization, programming, and structure of the church are not the end but only the means to an end—that of developing people into maturity and meeting their needs.

May God use the discussion of these basic principles to help us to develop healthy churches and, as a result, to reach our world for Christ. The church, by God's plan, sends maturing disciples to lost, alienated, hurting people to demonstrate before them changed lives and healed relationships, and thus to attract them to Jesus Christ.